## Acknowledgements

Previously published in:

"Peepers"
*Open 24 Hours*, Brescia University
*Love's Invisible Language*

Robert Graves essay:
*Legal Studies Forum*, University of West Virginia

"Adventures of the Shadow"
*Open 24 Hours*, Brescia University

"Victorious Horseman"
*Open 24 Hours*, Brescia University

"Indian Ponies"
*Open 24 Hours*, Brescia University
*Love That Moves the Sun, Broadstone Press*
*Love's Invisible Language*

"Our Garden," "Your Beauty," "We Dance," "The Fall Night"
*As If Suddenly Moonlight*


Cover painting by John Hay
Book Design Marjorie Snelson Design

Printed in the United States

ISBN 978-0-9988211-4-6

For information: jhay63043@gmail.com

# Love In A Wild Garden

## MEMORY, STORIES, POEMS

**John Hay**

# Table of Contents

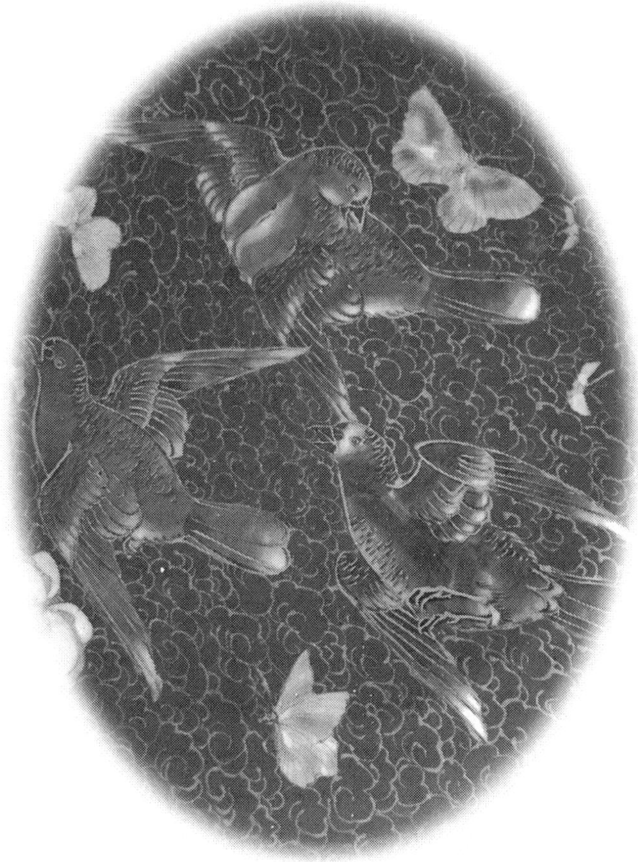

## Peepers

Your letter speaks of the inner universe; it is in the functioning of the means. We appraise and continue to sustain the many tiers of our travel. At sunrise, in the singing of the little frogs, the crickets' hymns, and the sound of the galaxies spinning, the secret is revealed – an internal secret protected by its demand for giving, and its immediate unlikelihood to exist.

Yes, culture will always leave home broke, and it breaks many. The ones it breaks are those who buy into their culture too deeply with the heart, because soon that culture will morph and die. Your letter is about spirit as a palpable force, like a touch on warm arms that respond. You write, "It was the insurgent breeze that touched me with feminine hands." Lovely way to say something that cannot be said.

And the little frogs! "We skip a rock over a pool of rainwater in the low meadow where the tiny green frogs sing flashes of mystical sound into the air, sing high-pitched change into the heart."

I remember that evening with you, skipping rocks on the wide and fresh pool of rainwater, a small sparkling pond in an emerald field. The evening light was blue and gold. Blue sky your eyes.

And the little frogs were singing brightly, chanting with us, setting up new pathways in our brain with transformative sound, pathways that lead to awareness and far-reaching happiness.

Those sounds cut into the moment, opening avenues within us. In truth, there is only the moment. And yet, the future leans against the moment and makes itself available to one who functions there.

Yes, Johnny. Yes!

# Mama Cat
# Some asked the cat: What Do You Hope For?

I hope for love, Mama Kitty said. I hope to choose slowly and be right. I like the rain and the way it sprinkles. (I don't like my vitamin, but we can skip that.) I like the sunlight when it comes through my eyes and draws me out into the yard. I like the little tub of water under the mimosa tree, where I lean to drink. I see the reflection of the clouds floating in the tree branches. I like my friend, Tabby, and Sheba too, who keeps everything full of fun. When Sheba runs up the trees for no good reason I can't help smiling.

We avoid the gray cat, except sometimes for Sheba, who is protected from his charm by her earned detachment, and love of play. We avoid him because deep down he is what he seems: angry and unaware. I like to sit on the cistern by the old green pump and stare at the white cottage where a gentle human lives. I like to sit in the window on the porch of the brick house and stare at the people inside. They don't do much, so I don't quite know why. Maybe I just like to stare.

I hope for Purina and not Science Diet. I like the visitor who lets me use him for a pillow at dinner after meditation class in the brick house. When the gray cat comes, I find something else to do. I could relieve the gray cat from a momentary desire for attention, but I could never help him, no one could. I hope for spring. I hope my friend in the brick house gives the rest of the

Science Diet to Tabby. Tabby thinks it tastes better when she is locked out late at night and is a bit hungry. I am looking forward to reading a book, learning French and dancing in the Peacock Palace. I miss Mr. Peep, the peacock. We often ate together or drank rain water together under the mimosa tree. As a snack, he would sometimes have a pink bloom that fell into the water. Mr. Peep was a good bird. He was gentlemanly and also spiritual since he was very young. His mom hugged him a lot. He was happy and at ease and liked to be around us. Sometime we would just stare together. He would go into a deep, restful, relaxed and peaceful state. In the spring, he would sing us all awake at sunrise. Thank you, Mr. Peep, for all your love. Thank you for making our eyes so bright. Thank you Mr. Peep. Thank you everyone.

## Essay On The Grape

When the bright grapes hung down through the wooden strips of lattice across the big stone posts from the vines in the sun, ripe and purple and firm and sparkling, we had to jump to bring them down. Grape jelly appeared in the kitchen with wax to seal the glass. Hot toast, butter from the cow and the churn, and grape jelly as sweet and true as the grapes that hung in the sun. And through the window the morning breeze is light and easy and touching sweetly in the mind.

Once upon a time in a far-off farm in Kentucky lived a youth who hoped he was destined to be, to live in the moment forever. Maybe all the way from heaven he found parents who would give inspiration and freedom to the youth in his journey, for it is a journey that he must make to reach the inner landscape. He knew very quickly that a grape was pure and that wine was imperfect and ineffective. He ate his toast and jelly as a child with one eye on the freedom of heaven on earth. He sought intuition wherever he felt it in others; or was it love and goodness that drew him. To recognize the right kind of persons and learn from them was a tremendous goal. There were the loved ones of his youth, there was a friend from far away. They helped him to question the seen and to seek the unseen. The grapes seemed to fall from heaven, purple and fresh.

The lasting grapes are the grapes of recognition and conscious change. From those grapes is made the Wine of Intelligence, the grapes from heaven. We jump to bring them down.

## A Friend In Robert Graves

We did not know where to live when we left Kentucky together for Europe, nor that we would find such a fine place to live as the all encompassing, Deya, Mallorca. I left the allure of central Kentucky, left a romantic, hidden farm strewn with animals and birds of all sorts, horses, donkeys, peacocks, guineas – and I left a helpful, lively, devoted family.

I had spent time studying English at the University of the South at Sewanee, in the mountains of Tennessee. Afterward, I took time to get a degree in law, that study made smoother by having read literary works at Sewanee in a critical manner.

When clerking for a year at Kentucky's high Court, a *Playboy* magazine was left on the chair in my office. In it was an article on genius by Robert Graves. His prose was clear and strong, his views personal. Graves, an Englishman, is often considered Europe's finest love poet. He is the author of over one hundred books, including *I Claudius, Claudius the God, Oxford Addresses On Poetry, Collected Poems*, a rendition in English verse of Omar Khayyam's quatrains titled *The Original Rubaiyyat*, and his controversial grammar of poetic myth, *The White Goddess*.

From his essay on genius, he seemed to be a different kind of thinker. The brusque manner in his thought was not unfamiliar to me. His prose implied an inner strength. I had not heard of Graves. My one reading of *Genius* was brief; the owner retrieved the magazine. His essay was later included in the collection, *Difficult Ques-*

*tions, Easy Answers* (1973.) Robert Graves seemed to be in a process of thought unlike that of the literary people I had known and studied. I was curious. What was his background?

When I lived in his village on Mallorca in 1970 and 1971, Graves was seventy-five. He moved like a knight fresh out of armor, as if still unaccustomed to freedom from metal and mail. His movement was full of life and charm, light really for his large frame. An old neck injury added emphasis to his conversations, as he would stop when walking and turn his entire body to speak, being unable to easily swivel his head far to the side. He was tall, maybe six foot three, near that, and powerfully built.

When I met Robert Graves he was barefoot, walking toward me down the narrow mountain road leading from the stone town of Deya to his home above the blue Mediterranean on the Island of Mallorca. He wore a broad-brimmed straw hat and carried a straw basket with long double handles that hung from his shoulder. He wore a white cotton, loose fitting, tunic-like shirt over white, loose fitting trousers. In dress, he looked very much like a local farmer of the island many generations before. He was tall, broad, and at seventy-five expressed an athletic, physical power. I could not mistake the force of his being, a kind and powerful intelligence. I knew I was in his village, and that he might be about somewhere. I knew it was Robert Graves walking up to me.

We were on the road to his home, Canellun. The mail was probably in his basket. It was September and warm.

He held out his hand.

"I'm Robert."

"I'm John Hay. I'm from Kentucky."

"Kentucky!" he said brightly. His eyes widened with that wonderful look of surprise and interest that brought a feeling that all the life around him had come alive. "Are you a colonel?'

I knew what he meant and smiled. "Yes sir, someone made me one of those."

"You outrank me," he said. "I am only a captain." And gently drawing himself up to attention he gave a quiet salute. As a captain in WWI he was immersed in the horrors of trench warfare. A Kentucky Colonel is an honorary title, given out casually.

I felt his kindness toward this young man from Kentucky, a traveler out on the open road. I felt his intense focus in the moment. It was as if I had come riding in swiftly on horseback, reining in a fast running horse, and Robert Graves had taken a strong hold on the reins, and given me a foothold down to the mountain road.

## Kentucky And Spain

On the road with him that day, that romantic mountain road, I did not know the extent of Robert Graves' reputation and work. I had never read a book of his, nor a poem. After reading the essay on *Genius* in my office, I stopped at the Louisville Public library and asked about him. The summer 1969 issue of *The Paris Review*, which included an interview with Graves, had just come out, and I asked the young, lady librarian if she knew anything I might read about him. She brought *The Paris Review* to me where I was waiting in a chair. At my shoulder she served the journal to me graciously. She laid it carefully in my hand open to Robert Graves' photograph, as if she were part of the message, as if Graves had meant a great deal to her. "He is a very fine poet," she said with warmth.

The particulars of the interview with Robert did not stay with me then. I did not encourage that kind of memory when reading it. My mind kept more to the sense of the man, his thoughtfulness and eloquence. And also the dynamic photograph in the café in his loose coat and long scarf and black flat-brimmed hat, with that now familiar smile of playfulness and acceptance and active interest, even as he stood quietly for a photograph. His smile, his brightness, that sparkle that would burst from quiet thoughtfulness, endured during all the time I spent with him.

Carol and I had traveled through France, Northern Spain, Portugal, Southern Spain, simply looking for a place to settle. I would be writing and she would be painting. In the summer of 1968 I worked as a shipping clerk in a Universal Joint factory on the south side in Chicago. My immediate boss was the brother of a well respected poet. He introduced me to him over the telephone. I was someday going to Europe to live for awhile and this poet spent time in Southern Spain. We went there. Yet, no place we visited was complete for Carol, and she was right; she needed the sea, the mountains, surroundings ultimately beautiful, and a community of friendly, sensible people near. To me that seemed too much to find in one place, yet I was wrong.

We pushed on to Palma, Mallorca where on a street corner we met a John Lennon look alike: round glasses, long hair, colorful, untucked shirt. Swinging our heavy backpacks to the pavement, and feeling the by then very familiar, always welcomed, relief from the weight, we asked him about a place to settle; he said that we should try the village of Formentor. He mentioned that Deya was a nice village, but added that the people there were unfriendly and would not offer a place to live. He had a feeling of kinship with us; as we did with him in a tender way, as he seemed lonely and lost. He said that the writer, Robert Graves, lived in Deya, but he was old and reclusive now and we would never meet him.

We learned later that the people who lived in Deya, during all or part of the year, artists and others with a flexible and natural sense of community and stability, had been disrupted during the sixties by people captivated by drugs, and the thoughtlessness that resulted. The people of the village were now careful to whom they rented houses. The next day we took a bus to Formentor. Neither of us felt anything to keep us there.

The following day we decided to visit Deya, regardless of what the young man had said; we knew by the brief meeting with him on the street we did not care to trust his experience of the people there. We bought a ticket in Palma on the roaring, rattling bus to Deya. It was an ancient bus with a long protruding hood which covered the motor. It was a faded brown color with a touch of faded gold – dating from the 1940s maybe. The old bus would slip out of gear on the mountain slopes, and would rush forward, almost silently, to unnerving speeds, and we would reflect hopefully on the condition of the brakes. Later we would see the bus parked beside the café in Deya the hood would be folded back and the Mallorchin driver and his friends would be leaning in with tools.

We passed Valdemosa where George Sand once lived. No draw to Valdemosa. It was like a movie set going by. Then came Deya, which was one of the most beautiful and inviting places on earth; circumstances there were right for us with our determination to explore inwardly, to live simply, to love, to work. We knew immediately: the blue Mediterranean below, the mountains above, necklaces of olive trees, a mysterious stone village with energy to clear the mind.

**Waiting In Deya**

"Robert Graves is senile. You might run into him on the road, but you won't understand a word he says." The one who spoke was a tall, handsome man of about forty with the kind of charm that searches for control. "I don't think he likes me, thinks I didn't treat a woman right who was here. I didn't do anything wrong to her, and what business is that of his?" He was one of the last people of the summer influx who were now leaving. He was the first person to speak to us in the café. It was probably good luck to be welcomed by a foolish man with the false message of Graves' early senility, a misunderstanding that still resonates in later writings about him.

The day we arrived, Carol and I rented a room in the little pension on the hill called the pooch. We would walk and explore or read in the day and sit in the café in the evening, hoping to meet someone and find a place to live. And now and then people would stop at our table to say hello. Very soon, as word naturally spreads in a small community, I am sure the entire village knew who we were. In less than a week a man who lived in the stark apartment in the upstairs over the Telephonos came to us in the café and said that he was moving, and that the Mallorchin lady, who was sole operator of this tiny telephone exchange in her home, asked that we visit her and talk. She was very kind, and we rented it that day. It was warm September. Carol and I were happy to be at ease and together, and we were inspired by the sky, the stone, the peace and quiet, and people who stopped to talk. We were twenty-six, learning what we could, and wonderfully optimistic.

"Colonel! Carol! Are you there?" It was our first week in the flat. Nightfall, a voice was calling up the stairway. It was Robert Graves, his first visit to see us. He walked up the steep, unlit wooden stairway calling again through the dark living room we didn't use. A small kitchen and another small room for sleeping was enough. "Colonel, Carol!" With him was a woman who was inspired by his poetry, and by *The White Goddess*, and of the type to set out on a pilgrimage to meet Robert Graves. She was from California. He brought her to politely leave her with us, so that she would not be left alone, so he could go about his life and work.

By then we were somewhat known in the village, at the post office that was in a small home, at the little store, polite meetings on the road; Robert Graves chatted with us one day on a hillside walkway down to the clot, the lower part of the village. And Carol washed our clothes outside by the main road with the Mallorchin women on the huge, rippling, waist-high stones with the water running over them from springs which came down from the mountain. She was the only non-Mallorchin who washed clothes there. Carol liked being outdoors in their company. She would talk and laugh with them without a bit of language in common, and they liked her very much, and all was understood.

"Carol, Colonel, hello!" I liked him; I felt I could learn from him, just that; I was very happy to see him appear in our apartment in his black horsehide jacket and colorful neck scarf and black hat, the same hat which I had seen him wear in his photo in *The Paris Review*, which he now politely removed. He was bright and engaging and powerfully kind. We had tacked a blanket in the doorway to the dark room to keep the kitchen warm. Ducking under the tattered blanket into the warm, candle lit kitchen, Robert Graves brought an impact of timelessness to the room, as if the present moment were our only birthright, and that in the tiny kitchen above the Telephonos was exactly where we were supposed to be.

He introduced us to the young woman with the hawk feather in her hair. I knew her by looking at her attire and her face and by listening to a few words. She was of the north eastern school's topical world by way of California. She had no interest in a friendship with us; we were not of her world. She had come for attention, a type of attention from Robert Graves that she would not get.

Robert Graves was all rhythm that night. He would quickly shift into the mood of the stories he told and the songs he would sing for us. His eyes would become bright, or very, very quiet as if he had shifted to a familiar state of peace. When he posed a question, a look of child-like wonder would follow, a look that was for us, the youth; he never preached. He smiled; he looked into the distance; he found interesting thoughts with a full, open expression of surprise and discovery, as if we had all found something very fine and necessary right along with him.

Carol and I were quiet people then, especially in the presence of those ahead of us in life, shy, listening, uninterested in pushing to express our own thoughts. I didn't make notes about my time with Robert Graves. I didn't need to make notes. The time is unforgettable, and so is the essence of what Robert Graves was then, was for us.

Robert Graves spoke of the olive wood we were burning in the small fireplace in the corner of the kitchen, which led to the olive trees and the mountainside terraces and their present state. He spoke of the village and the Telephonos below us, and gave us brief journeys into his life in the village, and he would interweave his thought with the history of the world and of himself; yet simple things, not heavy or impressive, just a fresh, creative sense of conversation to entertain, to love, to let us feel a little about himself. He spoke in a linear fashion when it was needed, called for by his simplicity in daily life, or out of courtesy, or to get the job done. Yet also, he spoke fluidly, as if painting in the wind with swift brush strokes the branches of a tree, interweaving.

Robert Graves brightly: "Would you like a song?"

"Yes."

Quietly: "Then I'll sing you one."

He had been sitting in one of the rough wooden chairs at a corner of our small table with a hand on each knee. His unassuming posture, with his hands on his knees, gave to the room a sense of calm. In his being he never got in the way of our inclination toward openness; he knew how to help us, how to offer just enough of what he was. The kitchen felt full of life, a dynamic universe all its own, put together with the blithe spirit of Robert Graves and our willing hearts.

For his singing he stood up quickly and took the three steps to the fireplace, turned his back to the fire and quietly settled with his arms at his sides like a tree that had been there for a thousand years. He did this a few times, singing very simple folk songs, often beautiful and poignant. To me he expressed the yearning of mankind to know the vastness of the universe, singing; no emotional outburst, no movement of his hands, just quietly letting the song come out simply and unadorned. With his arms at rest at his sides, standing in the little kitchen with the candlelight and the firelight, we felt he knew very much about the earth – a thoughtful man singing ancient songs of wisdom.

It was Willy what got drownded
In the deep blue sea.

Deep blue sea, baby
Deep blue sea.

It was Willy what got drownded
In the deep blue sea.

Deep blue sea, baby
Deep blue sea.

It has a meaning of a different sort for me now. I don't remember the part about the burial of Willy. It seemed rather sad then. I think there was a silver spade – something golden in there too.

Graves quietly and politely left us in the candlelit kitchen, and started on the two mile night walk around the dark mountain road to his home above the sea, to

Canellun. That was Robert Graves' first visit of many to come over the year. We walked with him to the top of the steps, leading down the dark, steep wooden stairway. I watched him leave alone in the dark. I knew a lot about him from that night. Because of certain people I had known, he was not all surprise for me, yet he brought together, confirmed anew, and lifted notches higher. His feeling said: the world is a place to learn and there is no nonsense in facing that intention; and happily, in that learning, there must be humor and play.

He left the woman with us, to whom we fed bean soup and salad; and, with little thought of recounting our own interests, we asked about her. She was pleasant, yet deeply and emotionally focused on the fleeting concerns of her culture. Robert was a force of the present that stayed with us, a present with intimations of the universal.

Deep blue sea, baby,
Deep blue sea.

**Yes Sir, Mr. Graves**

"Call me Robert."

"Yes sir, Mr. Graves.

We had been walking along the stone street to make another visit at mail time to the small home of Martin Talents, who was a master cabinet maker. I had by this time walked with Robert a few times to visit in homes around the village; or to sit with him while he opened his mail before our fire. Carol and I had left the Telephonos within a month to move to our newly rented home owned by a French woman who wanted us to stay there in the winter. The home had a huge, white art studio for her American husband, who was an artist. And

Carol had begun to make very beautiful batiks there in that finely outfitted studio, perched strangely in the upstairs of a traditional, stone Mallorchin home; actually three homes meshed together, with an indoor fountain, colorful tiles and Arabic archways.

So for the next few times together I called Robert Graves nothing, as I could not bring myself to call him Robert; something in my upbringing and sense of respect for the older man. Then one day.

"Mr. Graves..." I began.

He turned to me abruptly and looked down at me intently without smiling, meaning to end the matter and move on.

"Call me Robert. All my children call me Robert."

"Yes Sir." And little by little he became Robert.

Robert would often open his mail at our house, and take me walking with him after for visits to his friends in the village, or pick me up on the way to the post. I was the one interested in writing. Carol had other things to do with her art work. And everyone in the village loved her and asked her to visit. I was introduced to much of the village life because of the warmth of Carol, because of her draw to friendship.

**In Robert's Workroom**

Not long after, Robert told me that I could come to see him at his home at anytime. I was surprised and pleased to be told that, but I could not do it, that is, drop in on him uninvited. I think he knew that I would not abuse the privilege, and in essence he was telling this young man that he was accepted. Maybe I should have come for a visit a time or two, but I think not; I could have interrupted a poet who wrote in a very refined manner. Why do that? Anything I might want or need could wait.

The Kentucky poet, Jesse Mountjoy, a good friend at home, knowing I was in Deya, sent me a copy of Graves' *Playboy* Interview in the December 1970 issue. Robert had somewhere said that he agreed to the interview to teach *Playboy* a lesson. Maybe the lesson was something about romantic love, and the wonders it can work, as opposed to mere lust. From this interview, and in other ways, little by little over the year, I learned more of what Robert had done in his life.

I read Robert's novel, *Count Belasarius*, which was left on the floor in our apartment above the Telephonos by the last occupant. I read his book of poems from 1965 and his *The White Goddess* that were on the bookshelf in our second home. I made it through *The White Goddess* by enjoying the language, and mystery that lies beyond intellect. I quickly realized I didn't have the background or desire to embrace or enjoy the particulars of that intricate and inspired book. Yet, his premise is not complicated, though many of Robert's critics and competitors make it so. He uncovered in poetic history an inspiration for romantic poetry inspired by the Muse, an inspiration he recognized as his own.

I did not want to interrupt him by a visit. Anything I might want to say could wait. Yet one day he asked me how my writing was coming along, if it was going well. I was writing a fictional piece and now and then a poem. I told him that to write in the new house had been difficult. I said it didn't have a settled feeling writing there – something about it. Whatever the real reason for the struggle to write there – could I not have written comfortably in a vacant lot if my focus was strong? – the hard edge of the house seemed to intrude. Robert looked at me a few moments.

"Come to see me tomorrow morning. I have a place. I will show you." I believe that Robert was sympathetic, as he didn't really like what had been done to our new home. He didn't like the way the three old houses were put together and renovated. I could tell when he looked around. It was spread out inside, too much striving to be grand. Robert had a fighter's edge to call on when needed. A former soldier and boxer, he could be very tough in revealing what he saw as false in life. He could definitely frown. He would come forward to protect what he saw as threatened by the counterfeit in people or ideas.

In his offer to me of a different place to write, I think he wished to help me keep moving on in strength, to help me find the understanding available to me then. He knew he could engage my thinking with a shift in experience – another place to write – and he was willing to make the effort.

The next day, late in the morning, I walked to Canellun. Beryl, Robert's wife, met me at the door. She was welcoming and kind, but did not stop to talk. She took me directly to Robert's study. She opened the door and closed it behind me. It was my first visit there. Everything in his home was handmade, he told me, so as not to burden clear thinking.

He was at his desk, pen in hand, a pen of the old type with black ink near. And when he saw me there was no hesitation, the pen was down and he was up to welcome me. Seeing him there with pen and paper, in that study of old wood and books and artifacts and simplicity, I wondered if I should have come. I did not want to waste a moment of his time.

There was a shelf near his desk with talismans, different objects meaningful to him. He talked to me about each one. There was a small open vessel, as I remember it now, a mythical figurine holding a container on its back. In that vessel, or another, was a small amount of the magic mushroom which he had experimented with at one time. He had written about the experience and the abuses which were inherent. It was now only there for memory of the experiment. There were symbols attributed to the three-fold Muse, and other objects he has written about as signposts in his poetic journey.

In his bookcase were most of the books he had written. He pointed a few out to me, taking them off the shelf and handing them to me as he spoke. He showed me *The Nazarene Gospel Restored*, and spoke of the time it took to write it, and spoke of the man he worked with in writing it. He showed me a book he had written on English grammar, also working with someone else. I should study it now. And then he handed me a book with the title, *The Real David Copperfield.*

"I took out the adjectives", he said in a droll manner, "Made it better." And then brightly, "My most unpopular book. I wonder why?" And he smiled mischievously.

He then offered me a chair at a wooden table out from his desk. He laid a cloth book before me. It was a book of only one poem, written by an unnamed poet. Its width was usual, but longer in size than a regular book, and it had only a small number of pages. It felt ancient and handmade and was flexible in the hand. The colors were lovely and pale. I seem to remember that there was a drawing of a rose.

Robert left the room while I was reading. It did not take long to read. Maybe this poem is well known,

known to others, but I have not seen it again. It was composed of couplets in an old style, plain English words, no decoration, succinct and repetitive. One after the other, couplet after couplet, it named the things on earth that would die, animals, trees, the rose, all the beauties and the creatures of a magnificent earth, that they would die. And then, after all of that, all the melancholy of the passing of the charm and life of the earth, it ended abruptly:

> Man deceives death,
> After death he lives again.

He came back into the room, stopped close to me where I sat with the old book open before me. And like the book's last lines, Robert also said something final:

"Yes, it works that way."

## Sheep Herder's Hut

We left Robert's study and headed up a steep slope of the mountain, walking swiftly. It was steep, rough terrain, tumbled with rocks. I had come to visit because he had told me to come, that he knew of a place where I might wish to write. We walked in single file with Robert staying about twenty feet ahead. He walked nimbly and was never winded, nor in need to rest. I was not surprised really; endurance seemed to be built into him.

"Robert," I said, right at the beginning of our climb. "You just showed me your book, *The Nazarene Gospel Restored*. Should I read it?"

"No, too long. I'll tell it to you."

And without a moments hesitation he began to tell the story of the book. He would stop and turn in his quick strong way of turning and speak in a clear voice down the slope to me, always leaving off at an interesting place in the story; and then he would walk higher up, stop, turn to me and resume the story. Then he was off again briskly up the slope. Everything was alive, a story, a climb, inspired energy. As we reached the sheep herder's hut the story ended; I had nothing to add but a thank you, and we never spoke of the book again.

The hut was small, low, made of stones. It had one small room, rather dark. There was a table with a chair or two. It was the hut in which he had hidden himself away and written *I, Claudius* in three months.

He said that his home, Canellun, was mortgaged then and he had no money to pay the mortgage, and soon he would have lost his home. He said that he had a few books written on that time in Roman history in which he did minor research. Suetonius, I believe was one. And he added, that he had gone into a sense of the time and picked up the sense and particulars of the time and made a connection with Claudius. The sales of *I, Claudius* paid his mortgage. I did not ask what he meant by his back in time connection with the long dead Emperor Claudius, or how it was done. Of course his process would not be mechanical, but in the realm of the internal. I felt that if that were possible, and if my time to know would come, then I would know.

## The Thinking Man's Graves

One afternoon I was walking out the road alone when I met Robert walking toward the village. We spoke briefly and went our ways. Soon after, a large sedan, a black taxi from Palma roared up to me, coming from the village at top speed. A short, rather round man in a nondescript jacket and small hat jumped from the back seat to the road on the run. He was English. He was extremely anxious, out of breath. "I say, I need to find a bloke named Graves, Robert Graves, and I have to catch a plane. Could you tell me where I can find him."

"You know him?" I asked.

"I'm from Cambridge, I have an appointment to see him," he blurted out breathlessly.

"Well, you just passed him. That was Graves you passed on the road."

The man froze. His arms were at his sides, his shoulders tensely protruding upward. He looked down at the road as if he were staring at some gigantic beetle. His mind was processing. He had passed the tall, barefoot man in the wide, straw hat and rough white clothing carrying a straw basket over his shoulder. Could that be Robert Graves? Suddenly, he looked up as if he had just found the lost car keys in his pocket. And then, while on the run back to the taxi, "Right! Thank you. Goodbye." The taxi made a reckless u-turn toward the village. I saw the man's mind seem to go to that part of his research that billed Robert Graves as an eccentric, and then the light could go on.

### I Only Pose The Question

Now and then, not often, Robert would have a poem with him that he had just finished or he was working on, and would read it to me on the road or standing by a doorway in the streets. I later recognized some of these poems in his book: *Poems 1970-72*. It seemed that he did not read them to me for any feedback or even for comment, but only to kindly share with a young man who was writing and who looked to him to learn. And maybe to test the poems in his own mind out in the street, hearing himself read them aloud.

I remember a poem he read as we walked out on the road to Canellun. I would sometimes walk part way home with him and then turn back. He stopped. It was windy. He read his poem which ended with the question of who revolved around who, the man around the woman?, the woman around the man? Out on the windy road a multi-leveled poem, read once, can quickly pass on by. The poem ended with the choice between the two alternatives.

I asked, "Which is it?" He hesitated a moment, as if I had surprised him by asking for an answer. He spoke quietly: "I only pose the question."

**Your Own Voice**

"Robert, could you give me advice on writing poetry?" I believe that was the only question about writing that I asked him. It is the only one I remember.

During my time in Deya I had read very little of his work and little about him. I did not know all he had previously said about his poetic world in print. I was hesitant to ask the question. And now I am very glad I did.

After Robert had gathered his mail we walked down near the cafes. He had something to talk about with one of the Mallorchin villagers. The man saw Robert and came out of the café to the street to meet him. Robert introduced us. They spoke amiably in Spanish for a short time. Robert smiled and was cordial. Watching them solve a problem, most likely about some need in the workings of the village, it came to me to ask Robert about writing poetry.

I waited to ask about poetry until we were well free of the cafes, which were almost empty after summer. I asked. Robert swung to a halt and looked at me intently. The question was a powerful one for a young man to ask Robert Graves; poetry was the expression of his inner force, his engagement in words with love and the intuitive. And, in what he might call the Apollonian, intellectual sense as opposed to Muse inspired poetry -satire often – he used verse to call out the pretentious and the destroyers of life.

He did not hesitate with an answer; and I am sure his response was tailored to me and the time; what he felt I might then need to hear.

"Listen to your own voice," he said. "Robert Frost wrote that way. I knew him. His poems read like he talked. Listen to your inner voice and write, and it will be natural to you."

This is exactly the content of what he said and the brevity too. Then he spoke of E. E. Cummings and his respect for Cumming's poetry. He called Frost and Cummings friends.

"Eventually, you will write in a voice of your own."

Then he shifted his weight and paused.

"A person is a poet if they live poetically and never write a poem."

We walked on, and I felt he had given all I needed to know for the time. He gave me something neither too large nor to small for me to remember and aspire to.

## Food For The Ghost

One day, we were out on the road again. Robert was in his usual attire when the weather was chilly, corduroys, rough, brown coat and scarf and warm, wool hat with flaps swinging free at his ears. I was wearing, as I wore every day, a dark red, seven dollar, zip-up sweater from a workingman's store in Palma, under a gray, wool jacket. Once a week Carol and I would ride the old bus the fifteen miles to Palma and shop for only what was needed. We would go into the huge market with the gypsy women carrying babies, and Mallorchins selling vegetables and fish and every kind of meat, including rabbits and colorful birds. Carol came to know the Mallorchin women who sold vegetables from their boxes and baskets, and they liked her without having a language between them, and she would amiably go back and forth with them to settle on a good price. Liking her and smiling, they gave her exceptional deals. This was important because we needed our very limited money supply to last. We could live on fifteen dollars a week in groceries, and our rent was twenty dollars a month.

Robert and I were out on the road one day. We met a group of two men and a woman walking. They lived with a few others in a large, rented house in Lluch Alcari, a small settlement down the road from Deya toward the port of Sollier. They were "hippie" types, engaged then in 1971, like so many people today, in the delight for chemicals. The leader was a tall, slim man from Canada, of about thirty-five. We introduced ourselves around. Robert greeted them warmly, though he didn't know them, and he asked if they were doing all right in Lluch Alcari, if all went well. The leader then spoke to Robert.

"We have been wanting to talk to you. We have a ghost in our house. At night when we are asleep the ghost eats food from our cabinets. We don't know what to do. At night it is there, and in the morning it is gone."

Robert shifted his feet as he often did. The way he did it made one feel that he was extraordinarily alive and flexible in thought and that he was about to say something charming or profound. He then spoke confidently as if he happened to know the best and foremost answer to just that question.

"What you need to do is this," he said. "At the end of the day, just before you go to sleep at night, leave a portion of the food out on the counter for the ghost. The ghost will be happy to have received a share."

I could tell they were expecting a different answer, something more exciting, more mysterious. Robert was kind and chatted with them awhile about nothing in particular. He gave them his warm support. He knew they were looking to a man rather famous in their eyes, and he supported them in a simple, tender fashion.

When we moved on down the road he made no comment. He knew that comment was not needed.

## A Manuscript Or Not

Robert often took me to Martin Talens' house in the afternoons. Martin would serve us tea. Martin was about 50, not tall, a little heavy, with an intelligent face; and he carried a bit of tension with him. Yet he smiled often and was welcoming and warmly polite. Martin was very nice to me; I liked him. I seem to remember that Martin had put his home in England under the care of the National Trust. He was in Deya as a cabinet maker of the very highest order. He was then building a tall, free-standing Irish harp out of the finest woods.

Martin always listened closely to Robert in all he had to say and seemed to enjoy it. He encouraged Robert to talk on, and he made comments along the way. Robert often brought up subjects at Martin's house that seemed to fit with the settled time around his table, or the subjects were just good conversation over tea. The talk might start from something in Robert's mail, or his travels. I think he went to Budapest and London while I was there. The talk could be about the village, or about something Robert was trying to work out in his mind.

On this day he carried a long, handwritten letter he was about to post to Idries Shah. He began to discuss the letter with Martin. Martin seemed to know something about it. I did not know anything about Idries Shah or his brother, Omar Ali-Shah.

Edward Fitzgerald's rendition of the *The Rubaiyyat* of Omar Khayyam had always been on a table round and about our house on the farm in Kentucky, as had Sadi's poems and stories and an old, leather bound, abridged version of Sir Richard Francis Burton's translation of the *Thousand and One Nights*. My mother liked these romantic and spiritually engaging stories and poems, so she had them at hand around our home.

The letter from Robert was to encourage Idries Shah to produce an original manuscript of the *Rubaiyyat* from which a crib translation from the Persian, put together by Omar Ali-Shah, had been given to Robert to render into English verse. The book was published as *The Original Rubaiyyat*, and it caused a great stir among scholars and other readers who inclined to Robert Fitzgerald's translation and, most often, to his hedonistic interpretation of

Khayyam's poem.

The Shah brothers had not produced the manuscript, and had not clearly communicated to Robert their intentions. Idries Shah and Robert were friends for many years and Robert had introduced Shah to the reading public by writing the introduction to Shah's book, *The Sufis* (1964).

Robert had not seen *The Rubaiyyat* manuscript, but working from the crib, he wrote his rendition in English verse. He published the book with Omar Ali-Shah assuming the manuscript's existence. There was an outcry from scholars to see the manuscript, which was touted as older than the one Edward Fitzgerald used for his translation. The Shah family, Idries Shah and Omar Ali Shah, had not produced it. It was in question. There was an outcry that the manuscript did not exist, and that Robert Graves had been duped.

After Robert read a portion of the letter aloud to us, I remember Martin commenting:

"This will hurt your reputation as a scholar, won't it Robert, if they don't show the manuscript?"

Robert was frowning and nodded.

I got the gist of the conversation. I was merely surprised that someone in Robert's world of scholarship and learning might not be treating Robert honestly. I was surprised that he had to write such a letter to someone in partnership on such a level as those men seemed to be. I had no idea who they were, and I had no background with which to follow the conversation closely.

The manuscript hasn't been produced. Both Idries Shah and Robert have died.

I could speculate now, manuscript or not, that Idries Shah wanted the information out in the world that when Omar Khayyam spoke of wine and drunkenness, he wasn't speaking of fermentation or distilled spirits, and that it wasn't a document of "live for today" in the vein of the hedonist. What better vehicle to use for this than to follow Robert Fitzgerald. In the Victorian era the Fitzgerald version and the hedonistic interpretation of the quatrains swept over England, and are still very much alive. In the new version with Robert Graves's poetic rendering, the introductions explained that Khayyam used the word "wine" as a metaphor for spiritual force, and that the quatrains functioned in the long understood action literature of the Sufis.

**Christmas Morning Quatrains**

On the cold and cozy Christmas morning in 1970, the windows lit only by high, gray clouds, Carol and I were sitting up close to a blazing olive wood fire. It was cold in the large, stone room, and it was warm near the olive wood fire. The olive logs were cut from damaged trees, or from trees fallen in the natural decline of terraces no longer commercially viable. They were short logs, often twisted and thick. For us the fire was singing. Silence everywhere. Christmas!

We knew of no one coming to see us and we were happy to be there alone before the warm, sparkling fire. Out the windows it seemed that snowflakes drifted down over the quiet, stone village. Carol had made pecan cookies, cake, tea and hot chocolate, for us, and she made extra for anyone who might come to visit. She arranged them on the curved stone ledge, which was really a hearth of thin stones in grays and blacks, a handy shelf of stone at the low edge of the fire. We would both be very pleased if someone came by to visit on Christmas morning, yet we did not expect it. We had exchanged small gifts, and red ribbon was draped across the stone. We were content to be in Deya at Christmas with very little but ourselves. We were thankful and thankfulness was natural to us, and our feeling was gratitude for being in what seemed the simple, unencumbered center of the universe, and for the gentle truths and loving sense of Christmastime.

And in a while, in a voice not quite as insistent as usual, softened in the feeling of the morning, we heard, "Carol, Colonel, are you home?" As usual, he had let himself in briskly. We had no idea that Robert would visit, and it made us happy to hear his warm greeting. He was dressed in his horsehide jacket, black hat and a warm, colorful scarf at his neck. He came in fresh and strong, yet in a quiet mood, gentle.

He sat in a low chair which he pulled up close to the edge of the fire. He leaned into the fire. He had a book in his hand as a gift. It was his rendition in English verse of Omar Khayyam's *Rubaiyyat*: *The Original Rubaiyyat*, the book put together from the manuscript that had not been revealed.

He handed the book to Carol. He said nothing about it. He chatted with us a short while, and then he said goodbye to walk the road home to Canellun. I don't remember what we said. I just remember his quiet visit at Christmas and small talk around the fire. I remember the feeling of Robert walking away alone, as if we should have walked with him to his door, for cheerfulness on the road to Canellun.

We opened the book and on the first page Robert had written: "To Carol and John, with love, Robert."

We did not look at the scholarly introductions, nor

did we care. We turned to the quatrains themselves and read aloud, taking turns to read, one to the other. There was tremendous strength and beauty there, and an overriding sense that there was so much to learn in our life to come. These quatrains had always been in my home in the Fitzgerald translation, and I had never thought that Khayyam was depending on the beverage wine for his drunkenness. The poem just didn't feel that way. In those early days on the farm those quatrains with the "wine" meant the joy of life to me. Alcohol was popular in the culture of my early youth, but not in my youthful dreams. And it was not popular with us in Deya, nor after.

This time there was a knock at the door, and Vida Gabriella, such a helpful friend to Carol, came by with her friend and partner, Bert. Carol and I were friends with a number of people in the village who had lived there for many years. The people there that winter were artists and writers and those who loved the quiet, austere beauty of Deya, and all spoke English.

Vida lived in the village. Bert's home was a long walk out, overlooking the sea. Vida was dressed beautifully in a long wool dress and wide wool scarf across her shoulders and a long wool coat of muted green with gold. Bert too looked fine, dressed up for this special morning. Vida and Bert were writers, and they lived a life of simplicity in a very personal and unpublicized view of their art.

Accepting one of the cookies laced with pecans, which unluckily held a broken pecan shell, Vida took a healthy bite, and one of her front teeth broke off completely at the base. She was in the middle of telling a humorous story. She felt the tooth break, and calmly took it between her fingers. She looked at it briefly, and then quietly opened her purse and dropped it in. We were all quiet, watching. Without comment she continued her story at the place she had left off and continued to make it funny, and the tooth was never mentioned. Her smooth acceptance was a natural and gentle courtesy to her hosts, and especially to Carol who baked the cookie. It took a few weeks for her to have the space repaired, and she looked fine without the tooth. And without the tooth that Christmas morning, she did not change her smile, nor the humor in her story. In Deya there were people like this, people with strength and sensitivity, who had a definite regard for those younger than they were, with a desire to learn.

When Vida and Bert had gone, with logs still burning, and drinking a strong, black tea someone had given us, Carol and I read the quatrains of Omar Khayyam quietly before the hot fire. In the quatrains was a tender melancholy when the caravan of life is passing by, and generosity when the rose opened its petals to the wind, and romance when the lovers are picnicking in the free desert, and mystery when one more draught was asked for from the Cupbearer. We went right to what was given. Who would care in our state of being if a manuscript might exist or where?

We still do not care which manuscript is which, or if one existed and another did not. That is not our business. That is the business of scholars who try to keep things straight and create interest in certain fields of study. The content is our business and how we might use it to live.

The petals of the rose blow across the world, spreading gifts, generously, with largesse and laughter.

## Laura Riding

Robert had never spoken to me of Laura Riding. Someone in the village had given me a bare, skeleton story of Robert and Riding coming to Deya together in 1929, that she was a poet, and after some years, there was a final break between them and she had left town. In the talk, those who tend to make declarations about such things, it is said that she was Graves' first Muse. Who inspired who to do what in their literary efforts, seems to be a popular question as scholars and biographers rehash Robert's past.

It was late afternoon. The sky was full of color. Robert and I were sitting in straight-backed, wooden chairs on the flat stone terrace in front of my home. We could see out over a great part of the village. We had a fine view of the downward turning of the houses that were below us, tile roof tops, brown stone, narrow curving walkway. Looking out over the village, terraces with their high stone walls to hold the olive trees curved along the side of the mountain where the road from Palma lay quiet against the slope. A car was rare when the summer people had gone. No sound for a long time, no one walking, then maybe a muted voice from above or below in the spread of the village, and then no sound again; then the soft ring of a sheep bell from high up the mountain.

Robert had on his black leather jacket. His hat was beside him. He was relaxed and easy. We had gathered his mail in the little room in the stone home which served as the post office of Deya. He carried the mail at his side as usual in his long handled straw basket which hung from his shoulder. He set the basket on the stones, the mail in his lap.

His mail always had some letter with interest in it, and Robert very much enjoyed the constant stream of correspondence. He would read a piece of mail and then hand it to me. Some he would drop back in his basket. Some he would follow with a comment, from whom it had come and why, and some he would follow with a story. It was always a pleasure to be with Robert when he opened his letters. It seems that we were often out of doors or before a hot, olive wood fire at mail time.

He was going through the letters as usual, and I was sitting quietly, which was easy, natural for me to enjoy the surroundings and the weather. Robert opened a flyer of sorts, an advertisement, one of those pieces of paper that are designed in different type sets to market a product.

Suddenly, his entire body became alive as if all his muscles were engaged to move, as if he were an athlete ready for the whistle. He snapped forward with his elbows on his knees, the piece of paper held in both hands. He read it with a piercing concentration. He seemed to reread it, and then he leaned back. He leaned back at an angle in the chair, turning to me, and he looked steadily into my eyes without taking his eyes away as he talked. I remember it well, because it was a different look and a different way of relating between us. His look was as if something unexpected had happened. His expression was deeply thoughtful. He was doing something inwardly, as if what he read was being grasped as he spoke.

He handed me the paper, and watched me read it.

He immediately told me that Riding had left him and Deya years ago. He said that she renounced poetry and denounced it, that she started work on a dictionary with another man, and would have nothing to do with Robert or poetry. The notice brought news that now she was coming back to poetry; it must have announced her 1970 collection of poems: *Selected Poems In Five Sets.*

He said she had written some good poems before she had given up poetry.

"She took out all the poems that referred to me," Robert said. "They were her best poems."

Maybe he said, "Some of her best poems."

He left for home rather quickly then. He was still focused in the intense way that I saw when he leaned forward to read Riding's announcement. "Goodbye for now," he said. Then he shouldered his basket for the walk home to Canellun, a house he and Laura Riding had built when together. It was not my affair, and Robert was a strong man, but I felt a descent of melancholy as I watched him walk away, and something like melancholy left behind in the air. It was probably just me.

## The Tower And The Muse

The Tower was a house that Robert owned on the edge of the stone walkway just before the walkway turned downward to the lower part of the village. It was an upright Mallorcan building, nothing special on the outside, built of the brown stone with wooden doors. Our house, with lemon trees planted to curve against the hill, was the next house down, and our gardens came together with The Tower's Gardens.

It was springtime, and I walked out to buy something we needed at the little store. The red and purple flowers were blooming. The air was soft and sweet. The sun was bright.

Robert and Juli Simon were together in the small garden in the back of The Tower. He called me up to join them. Juli Simon, a ballet-dancer from England was the woman who was his Muse, to whom he was writing poetry, the last Muse. She was visiting from London to spend a few days in Deya.

I knew she was coming for a visit. From what little I had read about Robert, and understood of his feelings toward his Muse, I knew how much he must care for her and how much she must care for him. Robert introduced us, and I was, of course, the colonel from Kentucky. She was around twenty-one years old at the time, a strong, full, long-haired beauty with a steady, direct look in her eyes. She was gentle and well-mannered. She smiled freely, and we both laughed with Robert.

He was clean shaven and dressed in his black jacket and pressed trousers, a fine, soft off-white shirt and an especially bright, silk scarf tied at an angle at his neck. He wore no hat. He had a fine, elegant face. It was full and rugged. He had waves of white hair brushed back, which curled closely around his ears and collar. That day he seemed especially to shine, and he was full of playfulness in the flower-lit garden, a message of springtime. His Muse was with him.

He knew my birthday, and he informed Juli Simon that both he and I were Leos – lions he added – and he gave a mild, comic roar to prove it. He mentioned her sign and added some playful flavor with an uplifting thought or two of what her sign might mean; and I remember only our smiles and laughter. He talked a little about Juli and her dancing, and asked after Carol. I excused myself after a short time. As I walked away I could hear them talking quietly. With red flowers and sunlight, where else would they want to be?

The next morning as I was walking down the hill

along the side of The Tower, a window opened in the huge, flat, empty wall, level with me. The window was only a few feet square. It was a lone window, all by itself, as if it had no reason to be there against the big wall. It had a wooden shutter which opened outward. The sun was shining. It was Juli Simon who had opened it and was suddenly framed there, quiet and smiling, a portrait on the wall of a young, daring woman, very much alive, emerging into the sunlight from the shadows inside a tower. We chatted awhile, and I thought that if circumstances were different, if Juli lived in the village, that Carol would like her too, and we would be friends. I felt that Robert had good fortune to be with her, and that she had the good fortune to be with Robert.

**Time To Stand On The Road**

Robert and I were walking, and he stopped. He read a poem to me that suggested the oneness of time. He had been carrying it on a clipboard.

After reading the poem, Robert said: "Really there is no such thing as time. The past, the present and the future exist together. It is one thing."

"That is very difficult for me to understand," I said. "It is hard to grasp."

"I know," he said. "It's the strangest thing."

Time does not exist? Yet I was in another country. Carol was working in the white studio. I would be going home before long. Was that time? My time with Robert was only a small parcel of time in all Carol and I did and cared for in Deya. There were friendships, and cooking and the cafe and picnics by the sea. And for me, there was being alone in the sheepherder's hut or in the small back room at home writing stories set in my past in Kentucky.

Yet, I listened to what Robert said about time, and I was willing to live and wait to understand it, on its own level, if my time would come for that understanding.

**An Open Window**

In Robert Graves' life there was an unusual window from the fall of 1970 to the summer of 1971. And that window was open for me. He had time, and I had time, and for some reason he chose to give some of his time to me.

It was a miracle of sorts to rest in Deya. I was able to reflect on the influences which were forceful in my past, especially the positive ones: books of unlimited inspiration, beauty and struggle on the farm, loved ones who gave ease. In Deya, as in Kentucky, I had a clear intention to learn. In his life, Robert chose to embrace poetic understanding, spiritual force, intention, thoughtfulness, and the gifts of his tremendous discipline. I was fortunate to share some of that in action.

Looking back I feel that I understood what I needed to understand there in Deya; I did not wish for more. I did not make Graves a model, and never idolized him. I have never tried to follow in the footsteps of Robert Graves's poetic theory. He was who he was, surrounded by his world. His world interested me, but did not engage me to imitate it. His life force and his giving made a great difference. After leaving Deya, I read more of his work and life and the paths he took. I have written this memory especially for friends interested in my time with Graves, who requested that I write it.

When I returned to Kentucky, aside from some poetry and essays, I didn't study Robert Graves right away. I was taking care of a herd of Scotch Highland cattle and a herd of colorful horses in very rough country. We corresponded for a time, five or six letters. He answered mine. It was just news back and forth, and then he wrote that his eyes were bothering him, and he would not be writing again. His eyes probably were troubling him by then. Yet, he knew I was on my way, and his time was needed in other places.

When I left Deya I held the reins of a restless horse, restless to be off on the journey. Robert Graves and everyone who moved about in the village that year gave me a leg up. The horse leaps ahead, unsure of the terrain, yet with fresh food in the saddlebags: bright oranges, tangy lemons and red roses.

I could say it this way: Robert Graves was a seasoned traveler, looking to become the swim of awareness in the sea without shores.

Deep blue sea, baby
Deep blue sea.

# Two Waves In A Pickup Truck

Assured by grace,
Your hand light on the wheel,
The big truck rumbles;
Your earrings dangle; your hair tosses gold;
Your chiseled profile and soft skin
Alive with dancing-
The cloud world and trees tumble and sail by
On the screen of the window:
An outdoor theater of waves in the quantum field,
In the silence of the one great moment.
You smile and talk with me in space;
We are free together across the miles
- Immediate in the field -
Your eyes twinkle with light,
Angelic you are; your hair tosses gold;
Beside me, you, and the tumbling skies.

## Gethsemane

Carol and I visited Gethsemane in Bardstown one Sunday afternoon in November 1969. It was cold and the monks would soon appear randomly through the big wooden doors to sing vespers with the snow whirling against the earth-toned stained glass in the amazingly tall, slender church windows. Carol was wearing a fine, trim-fitting, three-quarter length fur coat she had bought in a secondhand store, and a long, red and blue silk scarf was tied loosely at her neck. She had long hair, in those days, that flowed to her waist. We were quiet in our feeling with no need to speak, and we walked slowly as if the white stairway were a garden path, and we were in no hurry. We walked up the white stairway to the balcony of the old, old white and tall and long and delicate, ancient church. It was very old and full of space, but it had been reworked and it was clean and empty and white. Our every step tapped a song in the air, and the door that opened above us rang softly and sharply. We were the only people on the stairway. No one had traveled in the light snow that cold Sunday to hear the monks sing vespers. We heard the door close, a ring of metal and stone. A strong man, solid in his build, a monk with gray hair dressed in his long monk's white and black robe. He was moving swiftly down the stairway. He had an intelligent, kind face, and he seemed confident, rather like a man of the outside world who was successful in what he had done. He slowed near us, and passed us and looked at us with a thoughtfulness in his expression, and a gesture of his eyes in greeting. When he turned the corner, and was on the next level of stairs, he stopped and looked up at us. For some reason, we had looked down, to follow him away I suppose. He seemed to be addressing himself to Carol when he spoke.

"Pray for me," he said. "I need it more than you."

And without looking to us for a response he was gone. We listened to the monks sing in Latin, the soft songs rising up hollowly against the stone. We liked the feeling of peace the songs gave and we liked them in Latin; no thought, just the beauty of the echoing voices in song. We drove home to a warm room and cooked something simple and ate quietly. We have not mentioned the monk who spoke to us on the echoing, white stairs of the monastery, yet Carol has prayed for him many times just by being alive.

# A Visit To The Prado

What a monumental world, visual art, the history of its making, its people and their lives, that record of tremendous human struggle. Being in downtown Madrid with time to spare, I thought of that struggle as I walked the half hour down the Paseo de la Castellana from somewhere around the Hard Rock Café at Margaret Thatcher Park to the Prado; not 13th century Madrid, but not far from it in contemporary strangeness. The ticket to the Prado was 14 euros. There was no one in line. It was a Thursday about five in the afternoon.

It was April and the sun was shining and the air cool, and the fine, tall trees, looking a bit like sycamores, in the center of the wide Paseo de la Castellana, lining both sides of the walkway, were breaking out with the pale green leaves of springtime.

The Prado, the building itself, is essentially rectangles and plain, inside and out. Inside along the marble floors and marble walls and columns and high ceilings of the Prado, in groups, were Spanish school girls, Japanese tourists, young couples from Spain and France; people of all ages were moving about, single, in pairs or threes or fours: Italian, Spanish, Russian, German, others; the young couples weaving about swiftly past the art, holding hands. There were people who stood to look at the paintings, and it was not a crowded time.

Yet no one stood before a painting for very long except where there was a low bench with no back, as there was before the huge Rubens. The Rubens depicted the birth of Christ with the wise men, and various characters depicted in the background – curious humanity – some looking at the baby Jesus, some looking at Mary and Joseph; and, here and there, looking at each other.

On that bench visitors would sit, some to rest, one man to read the morning news; and one woman only, stared intently at the painting. She was old and full around the middle and neither rich nor poor, but she looked sad as she stared up at the painting, as if in worship.

This painting is huge and strict and intense. I have always in my heart loved the Wise Men, The Three Kings, but these, in this painting, bearing their wonderful gifts, are too strong, too forceful to make us smile and relax in their presence. The baby Jesus is full of light and blends with his mother's light – an outsider's position because of his wonderful glowing inwardness – the outsider position warmed by spirit and his human love continued with him for the rest of his life. Mary's inner light shines tenderly toward her little child. One might choose to see Joseph as puzzled. It was very quiet there in the Prado.

Remember the love song, written nearly a hundred years ago, "Cry Me A River?" "You can cry me a river, I cried a river over you." The Prado is sad because of the paintings, because of the tremendous yearnings and difficulties of the people in the cultures that surrounded the artists in their time. "You drove me out of my head, but you never shed a tear. Now you say you love me; well just to prove you do, you can cry me a river, I cried a river over you."

The culture had leaders in those times with great power, who didn't fulfill their promises to their people, their promises of truth and peace, and this disconnect, however unavoidable, shows in the art. The people wept and moved away from that restrictive world, cultures defined statically by word and might and ritual. The people divorced themselves from all of it incrementally over time; and so the loneliness and the crying from being stifled and hurt, now shifted from them to the backs of those powers who had restricted their spirits with threat and false promises of peace. The paintings are tinged with sadness. The unconscious cultivation of sadness is a popular cult of human ignorance. All people want peace and love; they just go about it in ineffective ways.

"Cry Me A River" is a song that goes further than disappointment between lovers. It could be used to tell of the struggles of humanity with the inner self and the inherent anger toward the cultures that make promises of spiritual freedom, satisfaction, and personal happiness that are not kept. Could it be said that happiness and freedom from sadness and confusion must be earned in some way by each of us, with effort, and that the use of what is given is to transcend the gift.

There, in the same room with the birth of Christ, was a Rubens again, this time the story of the Choice of Paris; for Zeus asked Paris to decide between three goddesses – attractive, full bodied, mostly naked – as to which of them is the fairest. And the one he chose would get a Golden Apple thrown into the mix by a goddess sewing discord. The women seem to have a rather intense state of mind concerning this meeting, and they each offered Paris a bribe, promises of pay to be chosen. He threw in with Aphrodite and received Helen of Troy as his extra cash. And thus: the Trojan War to retrieve her by the Greeks. All of this for a Golden Apple and a contrived trade for an innocent woman! Not unfamiliar in the history of human greed.

Working at the foot of the painting, it was maybe

8' x 10', was a young man kneeling on the floor, an artist, around thirty, dark hair, casually dressed in jeans and shirt. He was on his knees, bent over, mixing paints. His face was near the paints – mixing from small glass containers in a wooden box with low sides. He was focused on his paints. He certainly knew a lot about them.

The canvas on his easel, maybe 4 x 3.8, was a copy of the Rubens, almost complete. His work was good. The skin of the people was fine skin. He caught, also, the egocentric, unconfident sense of Paris. It looked very much an excellent copy. Someone will buy, hang and enjoy having the copy; yet, it is difficult to be hopeful that the painting will uplift. Unless by a sudden realization in the buyer of the limitations in the work itself, of its burden, of the inherent sadness imposed. Ruben's mythic humans are in tension, defined by the intellect, not referring us to the force of spirit. Well, maybe the beauty of the women, their finely wrought skin as if laid in as fresh as an open sea. Maybe the goddesses, these ladies, were alive and happy and free before they stepped onto the canvas. Art can be a stepping stone to reality. Often, yes, but if art becomes, in reality, a boulder, fractured with intellect and ice, watch out.

Velazquez, Greco, Rembrandt, Murillo, Ribera, Rafael, and this Prado goes on. Technique is a wonder. Yet, the Prado does not have the feeling of a field or a meadow as the word, Prado, might be translated. The feeling of springtime rarely comes to the Prado. It is a wonderful museum to view what was done by artists working through the strain of culture. It is an old weather frozen in time for us. We can learn what was made then, even learn why, and be astounded by craft, yet heaviness reigns. The kings on their horses are lonely. Many of the women seem battened down. And yet, scattered, still alive across the Prado, the universal peaks through.

Wait! Goya! He was inspired to paint the eye of the Prado, the open window of its soul, its meadow in May. A painting that speaks true without posturing: The Naked Maja. Not a mere pretension of humanity.

While many paintings hang quietly alone, around The Naked Maja is a crowd of people seeming to be from every continent of the earth, from every country of the earth, flowing in to her. Most are impassive, but all are drawn to the ineffable. They stare blankly at her or at the wall or at each other weaving in and out slowly like gnats in slow motion, yet not leaving the Naked Maja, and when the crowd thins you cannot see it happen, and the crowd thickens and flows around her again as if from nowhere. It is quiet there. The Naked Maja is ensconced in a nook, The Naked Maja is alone. The small, three-sided room is a universe of its own. She does not grovel for a Golden Apple. She looks at no lover. But if she did, if she looked toward some lover in that artistically expressed deeper, spiritual state, her look would be the same: right through him. As a work of art, she is her own in the source of being, and that is all. Springtime comes to the Prado, by way of Goya.

# Olive Oyl and Marilyn Monroe

*Olive Oyl*
Frankfort, Kentucky

Dear Marilyn,

I write this letter because you asked me to write it so that you may show it to your daughter. You have told me she wants to turn her life around. You and I no longer need this reminder, these words, and yet some, who could be a great service to themselves and the world, will never hear them or make the effort toward love.

You ask me to write about my husband, Popeye. We live in the same world with Popeye, don't we, the world of the tiny, invisible things always on the move. Popeye acknowledged those little forces, made them his friends and focus, and used them to become huge. You and I, then, followed in his footsteps, and with his help, we too, became a center of the Universe itself. It is a quantum world. Yep, nothing solid about us, energy on the move.

You lived a creative and disturbed life, drinking and drugging and accepting unregenerate friends. You were wrapped up in sluggish habits. And yet, now you have changed, as I have. You did it! Even your memories have taken on balance; the harsh memories relegated to experience and understanding; and so in the neuroplasticity of the brain there is actual and positive change. Popeye, the first one of the Changed Ones in our circle, saw something possible in us. We have followed his footsteps to freedom.

It is a quantum world and a quantum body with

which we are gifted. Who helped Popeye to that high place? He never found a need to give her name, but help Popeye surely had. The quantum physicists write and talk and experiment at a distance, but they will never reach the final answer unless they jump off the sinking boat to swim with us. They don't acknowledge Popeye, or our reality, but only call it flaky and without accessible data. They think Popeye is a nice man, kind and bright, but Popeye's offer is unfamiliar and daffy to them; it is a focus that is neither in their training nor experience. They will not give up the iron leash of words or their separateness from the experiment. They think they are Popeye's equal because they are walking and talking and playing games of chance, yet in balance with the cosmic intelligence, they are not up to children aggressively and happily playing tiddlywinks.

Marilyn, as you are aware, I am not degrading physicists, or scientists, or anyone else or their families, I am merely talking of the possibility and the requirements of heading out toward human capacity.

Once upon a time there was a master of essential knowledge, and so, a master of himself – a changed one. He lived in a fine house for he had achieved in both the material and spiritual worlds; and, like others of this achievement, he had enemies of the kind who react angrily to what they cannot understand, or wish to have for free that which belongs to another. One day his enemies slipped into his house while he was away and left a poisoned apple on a table, where he would be sure to see it. And yet he did not die.

When he did not die, one of the conspirators who left the poisoned apple was so impressed that he confessed to the master his deed, and asked to study with him. "And please tell me," the reformed assassin begged, "How did you avoid death from such a poison as that?"

The changed one answered, "I am not in the habit of eating apples I find lying about the house."

Let this story tell multiple tales. Let there be a cosmic functioning in the story as well.

Let the story tell of intuition, too.

Does an invisible force of the Intelligence fulfill quantum expression? Quantum Physics is about the little forces that move within us, the tiny ones of which we are made, and the space between them. Think positively in life and the brain will begin to rearrange its quantum functioning. Make active forays inward and the ego will diminish and make room for love. When love expands its energy within, does a new and fantastic life begin?

The quantum world is the energetic world of which we are made; and, is there another nectar, sweet as hot honey, that unifies it all? That nectar will never be proved, only tasted.

Popeye and I have engaged this energetic effort together, and yet, at the same time, we worked as individuals. To understand the self there is the initial challenge of dealing with personal structures of ego and habit, those to be uncovered, and if false, discarded; the space opened is filled then with love. Popeye began first, and after led me with him. I learned because I was deeply interested, and willing to be inside the experiment, to challenge myself, to take the high dive into a new life of better understanding.

Marilyn, even though you depended on drink and drugs in the days of Some Like It Hot, you dropped it all, turned it around, and now you are a teacher helping others. There is no miracle better than that, and no better passel of miracles that led you on in your journey. Speaking of Some Like It Hot, you played a part that was generous and giving and true, and of course, you were wonderfully funny. Tony Curtis was a cad of sorts, and you were an angel. Remember the scene on the boat when you leaned in for that kiss? Your sincerity and strength and strong intention in that playful moment is the inwardness needed to lean into the knowledge of the self and engage the quantum world and beyond.

Hello to your lovely daughter if she is near. Could life be a playful, spiritual journey? We play and enjoy and understand.

Love always, Olive Oyl

Popeye just came home and sends his love to you. For dinner we are having steamed vegetables and sweet potatoes that are warm on the stove. Let Popeye's spinach be perpetual, invisible and always with him, giving him sharpness of eye and strength. See you Monday.

# Our Garden

Our garden
Needs nothing more
In this moment,
The only moment there is;
It blooms in the still night;
Wakeful
We come home to it,
Beaming love

## Adventures of the Shadow

Though it was the 18th of March, 1923, Johnny was a young swordsman on the high seas in days of old, wounded, fighting for life. A fever was in him, and his thoughts just would not work. He had a strong, fine, chiseled nose and hair that changed color in the light, swept back. The expression that held in his face was one of interest, restlessness and a bit of contempt. Some deep turmoil lay just below the surface, though Johnny had not gotten to it.

He is a swordsman without a sword as for him to be alive is to discover all that is true for life and death. He lives on the high seas, the high seas of the small town he was born into, as if sailing, vigilant in many weathers. He is of the days of old in that he hearkens back in history in his books and in his family stories and brings them forth in knowing and in wonder that there would be a time when 1923 would be the days of old to millions.

He is one to break through any barrier to answer his constant questions about life's mystery and meaning, especially what might be under a rock or behind a door, or in his weather worn heart of hearts. He knows that when you are very young and curious, the shell of a guinea egg is rock hard and bounces when you throw it against the barn, and that rabbits, when followed, circle back to where they started.

His well-muscled arm lay back on the pillow, too weak to bear weight. He was trim, yet powerful for his size, and becoming more powerful every day. His father would say, "Why, Hot Shot, you grew last week. Have you been lifting the buggy?" And they would laugh. Yet, as Johnny lay there in bed, he felt as if could not have lifted the yellow flowers that Leanna had left on the doorstep in secret. She had left them on the stone doorstep in the rain, and then she ran away through the side yard and on down Shelby Street, her blue coat and long curls flying behind her in the wind. Johnny could not guess that Leanna had left them, for he did not know her, but had only seen her in the school when he had spent a bit of time in school before leaving for New Orleans. In those glimpses of Leanna, she was another girl in passing, and he did not linger with it. She seemed delicate, pensive, and very lonely. He remembered her blonde curls across the paper when she leaned forward to write. It was the dark and dynamic Olivia of New Orleans who was his muse.

Doc Polsgrove stood up from Johnny' bedside, and did not say to Johnny that Johnny was going to die. He did not say that Johnny's death could come soon, or in an unknown stretch of time. The doctor just looked down at Johnny kindly, took off his gold spectacles and wiped them with his white handkerchief, and asked Johnny what things he liked to do in life. From the fever, Johnny's head turned from side to side on the pillow. He would not remember what he said.

"I want to break my new horse to ride," Johnny said with strength, forgetting that he was weak. "And I want to learn to shoot straighter, so I can find some food for myself like my great grandfather did. And I like to go places alone."

"Alone?" The doctor looked away to the high ceiling, feeling such love and compassion for Johnny.

"You know, without getting in trouble for staying out alone. I am a man now. And I don't need someone else to know where I am all the time. I want to go places and understand what is there, not just to sit around until I'm old, listening to gossip." Johnny trusted the doctor, and though he felt unhinged by the fever, it was his pleasure of the moment to tell the doctor his thoughts.

"Well, son," the doctor said, smiling, "gossip can teach you about people, whether it is good gossip or bad gossip. If you know the difference."

Johnny searched feverishly with his eyes.

"What about school?" the gentle doctor asked. "Do you like school?"

"Not so much," Johnny spoke haltingly. "I guess I haven't really been to school here in Kentucky; a couple of years ago I went – for a few weeks. During the school year we go to New Orleans where my father works as a judge at the racetrack. I have a French girl who teaches me there. Olivia. She is nice. She is pretty. She likes to do things, interesting things. We go into the woods and hunt for snakes and take a boat into the swamps, walk around in the French quarter, eat ice cream in the cafes, eat Cajun food. She likes the cafes and the plain restaurants where the workingmen go, the metal workers and the dock men. We sit at a corner and talk. No one seems to know we are there. I can speak French pretty well, and she speaks English – so beautifully – you know, different, like she is speaking a poem. She likes books, too. We read together. She is eighteen. I am almost sixteen."

"Do you have friends in the school here in Frankfort," the doctor asked nonchalantly.

"My parents put me in school here for a few weeks at the end of the year one time. The kids laughed at me in math class because I didn't know how to do it. I know stories, though; I have read a lot of them. Then Jasper beat me up, so my mother took me out. I will thrash him good one day. I will be tougher than the toughest."

"Jasper? Who is that?" the doctor asked. Yet he knew of Jasper and his family. He knew the mother was addicted to heroin and the father at the least to alcohol, and that it was rumored that the father bought heroine and other drugs from the gypsies, and sold to anyone with a bit of cash. The doctor knew that the father encouraged Jasper to fight, and taught him to get what he could, though Jasper's father had a lumber yard and made good money. The doctor thought Johnny might want to talk about it.

"Jasper is bigger than the rest of us," Johnny said. "He's stupid, but not about some things. He lies, and a lot of kids believe him. He picks on just about everyone. He makes fun of girls."

"Well, you're old enough to ride a horse, and I bet you will be a top notch shot. And you are already a reader of fine books; I've heard that."

"Yes, sir."

"Drink plenty of water like I told you, Johnny, and get up from bed anytime you wish, and do anything that you might like to do. I will tell your mother you can."

Something moved deep in Johnny's chest; something in the doctor's words released him. Johnny began to cry, as if deep within he felt a sadness coming to him from the doctor. The doctor had already turned away, scooped up his broad-brimmed, felt hat and opened the door with a rustle of brass. The doctor's words spoke of a freedom unknown to Johnny. It was a freedom knocking on a closed window deep in Johnny's chest.

The doctor went out into the hall and shut the tall, wooden door behind him.

Johnny's mother was youthful in her look and youthful in the quick, graceful way she moved, and her nervous temperament was artistic. She made paintings of the Kentucky River and of anything about her that caught her eye. She made small, life-like sculptures in clay with her hands. She made anything that came to mind – a cat, her husband saddling a horse, of Roller, Johnny's hound dog, a lion leaping in the air, anything. All she made drew the viewer's eye to its humor, its strength and its reality. Her hair was swept back with a curved, tortoise shell comb. Her hands clasped in front of her waiting for the doctor to tell her about Johnny. For all her skills, however, she had a nervous temperament.

The doctor was thoughtful and tender with the feelings of Johnny's mother, and he took a long time to tell her that Johnny had a certain fever, a rare disease, and would not live. That he may get up and seem fine for a long time, maybe even a year, but that he would die. And he took a long time to say, "Don't bother to send him to school. Give him a horse and a gun and let him roam and hunt as he pleases, if ever again he feels like roaming."

"He's a brilliant child," the doctor said. "And the light in his eyes is brilliant. Maybe he sees more than most. There is something very old in Johnny. He seems to have been born young and old at the same time. Maybe he sees more than you and I."

This last part about him being a brilliant child, Johnny did not hear, but the first part, when the doctor told his mother that he was going to die and that there was no need for school and that he should be allowed to roam free, Johnny heard clearly. In his fever the part about the horse and the gun was at first more interesting to Johnny than the doctor's awareness of his impending death. He could understand a horse and a gun, but not his own death.

He followed the doctor to the door and turned the brass knob gently, as he wanted to go outside to check on his hound dog, Roller. He stood for a moment with the door open a crack and heard the doctor's words. Then he went back to his bed and began to cry. He didn't know why he was crying? It didn't seem then that death frightened him; it was just that he didn't want to miss all there was to learn. He buried his face in his pillow and cried until he fell into sleep, restlessly, with his mother at his side.

## Johnny's Battle: The First of Many

Johnny was not yet called the Shadow, not yet. He was feeling better as the doctor said he might. He stood in the window of the stone cupola, a turret, a watchtower atop the tall and ancient brick farmhouse. It looked like a minor castle or a hideaway for a mysterious thinker with exploration in his blood. The farm with its home was named Point Breeze, for it sat on a very tall hillside that overlooked the town, and it seemed that always a gentle breeze was blowing in summer and chilling breezes in winter that made one wrap a wool scarf a little tighter against the cold, even inside in the big rooms when the fire had burned low.

Johnny was feeling better, as was not unusual at times in the progress of the fever. Johnny felt like going out alone. He climbed the steep ladder into the cupola he liked to call The Tower. Its window was shaped in an ancient architecture with curved stained glass at the edges, as if from a church – an arch from some distant, arcane,

Arabian architecture. Johnny looked out over the town of Frankfort, Kentucky, as a knight of old making his plan, a knight accepting his fate to travel out and do good works in the forests and the towns of his countryside. A yellow finch lit on the windowsill and helped herself to the crumbs Johnny put out for the birds. He liked to watch them jump and move and turn and fly. He knew they were tuned for survival.

He could see the Kentucky State Capitol's huge, triple domes of limestone and its great, limestone wings of offices where the lawmakers worked. It was a graceful building finished in 1910 three years after Johnny was born. The American flag in front of the capitol was folding and unfolding in the breeze. It looked no bigger than a postage stamp from Johnny's tower, yet he saw it as bright and optimistic, a reminder of goodness in his own land.

The capitol was finished in the year Halley's comet streaked across the sky, the year Mark Twain passed on, and all who were prepared for Halley's comet looked up. Those, that is, who were already looking up, wishing to explore and learn about their life in the world and perhaps to study their inner being.

The ones looking skyward might be lying on a roof in the moonlight, or taking a buggy ride, or leaning back in a wooden swing on an open porch. Or maybe two affectionate souls, touching hands, were just lying in the grass on the lawn looking into the night sky, for in some mysterious way, the night sky had beckoned them to look. The comet's tail was 24 million miles long, and the Earth passed through it like a tiny spark. Even though he was only three then, Johnny remembered being held by his mother, wrapped warmly in her arms. She was sitting in the buggy where it was parked for the night without a horse. He remembered her warm arms and the blanket and the breeze. He could feel they were watching for some angelic offering from the sky.

Some are afraid of a comet's coming and think that a comet will bring ill fortune. On the other hand, some believe a comet is a sign of a great happening on the earth, as if someone watching it pass will find a difference in life itself, a positive difference that spreads out in ripples in the universe forever, to help all people over time. The doctor wondered if Johnny was one of those who were born to make that difference.

So I am going to die, Johnny thought. Yet everyone is going to die. The difference is that I feel it. Doc Polsgrove said I was going to die, maybe soon. I heard his words. Maybe I will do some important things before I die. But what could I do? What would other people do if they thought they were going to die, yet they felt pretty good as I do, as if I am going to live? What would the beautiful Olivia do for herself down in New Orleans?

Hearing an unfamiliar sound, a knock against wood, Johnny glanced again out the arched tower window etched in green and gold, and there was Jasper throwing guinea eggs against the side of the barn. Holt was with him, hunched down on his knees, handing Jasper eggs from the guinea hen's nest. The eggs were bouncing off the wooden planks of the barn. Not one egg had broken. Holt was heavy, too heavy. Johnny saw the guinea hen fly to the paddock fence with high-pitched screeching as only a frightened guinea can screech, like the frantic sound of a phonograph needle raking across the grooves.

Johnny ran down the stairs swinging against the banister in the curves. Jasper is too old for this, he thought, but plenty mean. He saw a vase of yellow flowers and a mirror flash by. The air was warm and swept over him. He was barefoot. His mother was at the bottom of the stairs with a watercolor in her hand. It was a painting of a pool of water reflecting the sunrise, and there was a rabbit jumping into the air. As his perception morphed into slow motion, he saw deeply into the painting. He felt the quiet pool of water of the painting relax something in his being.

"Stop, Johnny," his mother said. "What are you doing? Come back here."

But Johnny swung open the door and was through the yard in a flash, running and jumping rose bushes. He gave a flying block with his shoulder, and Holt, who was still kneeling in the grass and weeds by the deep, guinea nest with an egg in hand, rolled over twice with a scream and a groan. "You busted my arm," he yelled. "My arm is busted. Damn you, you little bastard."

Johnny rolled once, bounced up, and charged Jasper who was glaring at him, fists clenched. Jasper stepped back and hit Johnny a glancing blow to the head. Johnny reeled and staggered and finally caught his balance against the side of the barn. Then he charged, head down for a low tackle, and Jasper caught Johnny with a hard, chopping fist to the jaw, and Johnny hit the ground out cold, and he did not move, his closed eyes facing the sky as if he were napping on a summer afternoon.

Johnny's mother came running across the yard, almost as agile as Johnny had run, and she brandished a heavy cane. It was a decorative cane with a carved alligator and a carved frog on its shaft, a cane to let them know she would protect her guinea hen and her son. Jasper picked up two of the eggs, and smashed them together with both hands, and dropped the broken shells and egg slime into Johnny's upturned face.

Jasper and Holt took off at a run, crisscrossing the small field and out to the tree-lined road, then to the hillside off Shelby Street to the town. Johnny's mother stopped and leaned over Johnny. "I'm okay," he said. He slowly sat up and wiped the egg slime into his hand and onto the grass.

"Good for you, Johnny. He is bigger than you, and a fighter too, you know."

His mother – her name is Eugenia – gathered all of the guinea eggs that had bounced off the barn and put them back in the nest. "The hen will come back," she said. "Guineas are not that particular about someone touching their nests, you know. The boys didn't realize how hard a guinea egg is to break, did they?" And she laughed.

"I'll fix them," Johnny said quietly. "They'll pay. Jasper and Holt will pay."

"What do you want to do to them, Johnny? How will they pay?"

Johnny was taken by surprise at her question. All he could manage was to put a threat in his voice. "I'll give them what they deserve."

"Like what?" Eugenia asked.

"I'll knock them out."

"Can you?"

"Whose side are you on?"

"Your side, son."

"If I don't protect myself they are going to get me."

"I won't argue with that."

"So?"

"There are many ways to protect one's self," she said. Her voice went very low and quiet.

"What are they?" Johnny asked quickly, as if he needed to hear them and get to work.

"That will be up to you to find out," she said. "Won't it, son?"

Eugenia put her arm around Johnny as they walked between the flowerbeds toward the house. The jonquils glistened.

"I have heard about those boys, and I know something about their families," Eugenia said.

"You do? What have you heard?"

"Maybe you should avoid them. What I know is merely what someone told me, what someone told to them, so, gossip of sorts. Drugs involved, anger, brutal treatment of the innocent by their father and mother. It seems you should avoid these people. There is plenty of room in a small town for everyone."

When Eugenia thought of her own words – "plenty of room," she could scarcely believe them. They were words of an idealist, and though she knew she inclined to the ideal, she was not an idealist, not one of those characters who winced at common sense. A practical idealist, she thought, to give herself a little credit. Credit she was not sure, in this instance, she deserved. "Maybe not the actions of everyone," she backtracked.

"I don't quite know about that," said Johnny, not believing at all that there was always room for everyone and everything – not room for the bad, he thought, the bad just muscles in and destroys.

"You did good today," Eugenia said.

"I did? How?" Johnny frowned. He was having none of it.

"You protected the eggs of our guinea hen, so she can have young, live on, do what she is supposed to do."

“Maybe,” Johnny said without emotion. He gave no credit to himself. He was thinking of the future, what he must learn, and fast.

**That Night**

Johnny’s family met together in the living room for conversation about all manner of things. They met in the evening after dinner on nights that were free from family needs and their work. They talked literature and politics and all aspects of culture, yet more often, about life on the farm, the horses and the milk cow, and the goings on around Frankfort. They told jokes, and though some might be bawdy when only the men were there, the jokes were never cruel or unclean, just clever or full of wonderful nonsense. The family went to bed early on weekdays usually, but on weekends they would gather in the evening, and they would invite other couples, friends, cousins, aunts, uncles, storekeepers, neighbors – and those who liked the feel of things in that home would come; and they invited those shy or restive ones, who didn’t like society so much, but who seemed to have a need for company.

Johnny grew up listening to these evenings of talk and laughter, as a small child lounging under the piano where he would crawl. The grownups would forget he was there, and he could stay up late unnoticed and hear stories that would otherwise be kept from him.

When he was very young, the voices would lull him to sleep in the underbelly of the piano, but as he got a little older, he began to find meaning in the conversation, and very soon his ears were open for knowledge of the grownup world.

When he was too self-conscious to crawl under the piano, there was a small wooden chair, intricately carved with deer and eagles and angels with faces alive and mysterious, as if they were encouraging life and learning. The chair had a faded red, cushioned back. It looked as if it came from a formal castle or from a church where a preacher might sit between hymns. It was partially hidden by the grand piano top propped up, and Johnny would think himself small in that chair and would soon be forgotten by the others. The family and their friends would talk, and Johnny would listen. They often spoke pleasantly and interestingly on many subjects, and there was a feel of ease and trust and sincerity that kept Johnny in touch and thinking.

On the night after the fight with Jasper, Johnny was in a chair holding a book, bored to be in his own room, wondering what thoughts were coming up at the gathering downstairs, and wanting to feel the warmth of friends. He did not want to sleep or read; he was charged to be alive; he sensed the time called him for something more. There were seven friends of his mother and father visiting for the evening, and all were entering into the conversation. Only a lady in red saw him as he took his seat behind the piano from where he listened to the conversation:

"Listen, this is the 1920s; everything is changing."

"Already changed, you mean to say."

"And changing."

"The skirts are higher."

"Fancier. No sleeves."

"Yes, getting sleek."

"You mean chic."

"Sleek and chic."

"The war changed everything."

"It helped women."

"In what way?"

"They feel their beauty and their strength."

"What is that supposed to mean?"

"I know what it means."

"Tell me."

"Find out for yourself," Eugenia, his mother, said, and she laughed.

"So what women do you hearken to in the culture?"

"Hearken to in spiritual seeking, or in culture?"

"Culture. Society."

"How about Nellie Bly?"

"She was before the war."

"She faked insanity to enter a women's asylum in New York to report on conditions there. Judges and finally doctors, all men, judged her insane and committed her to the asylum."

"I remember it, too, from the newspapers. Didn't Nellie Bly conclude, among other things, that anyone, even a healthy woman, would become deranged in three months under the harsh treatment in the asylum?"

"Exactly."

Johnny was listening with passionate attention. He had perked up when the subject of women and their dresses came into the conversation; he was sixteen and feeling their draw. And he hated worse than anything for a girl or woman to be hurt or mistreated. When the power of his attention was turned on, there was nothing that could divert his mind

At sixteen, young women, and girls older than young, had been on his mind for a number of years. He had been in love from a distance, now and then, since he was seven. It might be a girl he merely passed on the street, or who was at another table in a restaurant, but love it was to Johnny. These girls he loved had something in their kind spirits that swept over him. He couldn't figure how they existed in such a rough world. He watched adults and felt that in most of them the child was gone, the flavor of flowers was gone, some charm that was visionary was gone; though he didn't know to say it, and so he did not think those words, he felt them. He hated Jasper for verbally abusing the girls at school. He feared what Jasper might have done to Mary Ann.

His tutor in New Orleans, Olivia, had seemed so much older, and she had a casual way that held always the feeling of a teacher and a pal. So Johnny had only respected her; yet now, as he was growing up, flashes of her graceful legs and full lips became momentary disturbances. She had that sweeping spirit, a brightness that overwhelms, as if it were something she was born with and that she continued to protect with her habits, and to earn.

And yet, Johnny's family not having traveled to New Orleans in six months, Johnny began to realize that she was merely a year and a half older than he was. He also was realizing how intensely he was missing her, and he kept seeing in his mind's eye that sultry afternoon she got up swiftly at the restaurant where the waiter put fresh newspaper on the tabletop and turned over a round, tin tray heaped with deliciously cooked crab onto the newspaper, and the tray had been previously used to serve drinks, and it was in a stack of trays unwashed and the cook in the workingman's restaurant had picked up the next tray and covered it with the wonderful crabs which were turned over on yesterday's newspaper, and Johnny and Olivia had dug in with their fingers and smiled happily at being alive together. And it was the loose summer dress that she had pulled up in the heat, and the way it came high above her knees.

And the time on the creek bank, turning over rocks with her looking for crawfish, when the top buttons of her blouse had come loose, and the buttons were left open, unknowingly, and sweetly unattended. Yet his mind, on most of the magical days they spent together in the cafes or under the warm Louisiana sun, kept her close in his heart as his older friend and teacher who was kind and knew about so many interesting and rare subjects, from turtles to jazz, and shared them all with him as if they were pure gold. One night she took him to sit under the window of a bar where the new jazz was playing. They leaned against the wall and peeled oranges she had brought. She was wearing trousers and had her hair pulled up in a yellow cap. The wall was made of planks, and the white moon was a sliver.

And in his home, as on this night, Johnny listened to his family and the guests, and watched the gestures of these men and women from many walks of life, heard their frequent laughter – listened.

"Why don't you serve a drink or two to your thirsty guests?" the gentleman who owned the hardware store asked playfully. "Before prohibition, you always regaled us with a drink. It's easy to get. Where's your good cheer?"

"What good is it?" someone asked.

"You got me there," he said.

"Let's change the subject," someone said. "That is an old boring one. Let them get drunk in the speakeasies in New York. They feel like they are doing something."

"The speakeasies sound fun to me," someone else said.

"Makes the girls happy."

"Only in Paris."

"What do you mean, makes them happy?"

"My aunt became addicted to heroin in Paris in 1901. She is dead now."

"Dr. Polsgrove won't prescribe it except for extreme pain."

"How did it affect her?"

"She needed the drug. It was her pleasure in life. When it was no longer available here over the counter, she had a hard time. Died of an overdose of it, it seemed. She was living alone."

"So sorry," someone said.

"Yes," Johnny's father said. "We liked her very much when she visited us here. She always brought eggs or flowers."

Johnny had heard the story of her addiction and death. He also had heard that Jasper gave some drug to Mary Ann at school. He heard someone say she quit school, lost interest. Johnny felt a sharp pain in his chest for Mary Ann, though he did not know her. Her name, Mary Ann, so gentle it seemed to him, and what Jasper did to her brought a pain to Johnny's chest. He shook it off and listened.

"Paris is the place to be for women," someone said. "For an American, that is."

"Right. Just up and go to Paris. You're dreaming."

"Paris is always in the papers. Has been since the war."

"Expatriates."

"F. Scott Fitzgerald!"

"His books are very limited."

"Right. Fitzgerald!"

"No, before that, much before that, people from America have been enjoying Paris."

"Your son is living in Paris, studying there."

"Right. I miss him. He is doing well it seems."

"People go to Paris and do what they want."

"What do they want?"

"Well, they explore their consciousness."

"And their sweethearts."

"Young people, who are restricted here, are free and loose there. Not your son, of course."

"He doesn't report everything to me, naturally."

"Yes, during the war. And now."

"Our soldiers, our boys, have brought it home."

"And the women who worked in the war, the nurses, and all the other jobs they filled, and the freedom of being a thousand miles from home."

"What good does it do them?"

"Pardon me if I say sex is a draw."

"You are not pardoned."

"For the men, the ladies of the night."

"Too simple. There's courtship, you know. Women are half of it."

"Let's change the subject."

"Have you read Fitzgerald's *The Beautiful and Damned*?"

"You believe that stuff?"

"Merely a take on the east. People on the wrong track: the confused and the pessimistic. Too much in the mind there; false intellect, you know."

"He makes it up for his career. Really it is just a composition; his troubled life is in it."

"Career?"

"Writer."

"I've read the book and the other one. Not much. You could be right. Yet, things are changing, regardless."

"Books."

"Right," said one of the guests. "Yet my son tells my wife and me stories of Paris, and I have been to Paris. I have bought tickets to go back. And have we not seen the changes in dress and thought – and morals as some people express it – that the soldiers are still bringing home. And we see it from the girls who worked in Europe in the war. Boys and girls are not books. The Europe that shocked them is not a book."

Johnny was inspired, shaken, bursting with excitement. It was if he had heard of worlds that he could not imagine being real. He had been reading between the lines as they talked, and whole worlds opened in him like wakefulness from sleep, as if he looked into his future, as if he were out there in what was to happen; it felt to him like love. Johnny had read many books, and many of them were set in foreign lands. But to hear of Paris and about a war he had heard of so often, for so many years, and of changes in the entire culture filled him with excitement and impatience to live on. He was hearing everything in his life differently. He was growing up, yet he was going to die. He thought: Who would ever really know that one's own culture was changing like the rustle of leaves above one's head before a storm. I don't want to die.

Johnny stood to excuse himself to the company and his family.

"I am sorry to interrupt," he said to the gathering of guests. "But I have some things to do. Thank you all for coming. I will see you next time, I hope. Good night, Mom and Dad."

His mother looked at him, and she was sorry he

had no friends in the town, sorry that the family spent so much time in New Orleans, and deeply unnerved to think he was going to die.

"Good night, Johnny," she said. "Good night, son."

And the rest of the people wished him a good night, and when looking at Johnny, something in them was stirred, and they meant deeply their good wishes for him.

"Yes, good night."

"You are a fine young man. Good night."

"I didn't see you there! Good night."

"You are like a shadow."

"Yes, a shadow.""We will call you Shadow."

"Do you mind?"

"No fine." Johnny smiled. "Good night."

"I didn't see you either. You must be invisible."

"Good night."

"Good night."

Johnny speaks to them kindly and sincerely, and smiles. He feels the love for them he has often felt over his life for those adults who graced his home. Yet suddenly he takes notice of that love with a jolt of recognition that the feeling of love has no clear boundary or definition but like weather covers all of them and everyone he knows and those he has never met.

Johnny walks through the wide hall into the library. The books are flattened to the tall library shelves by the moonlight. He smells the faint, soothing odor of the outdoors. Through the trees, the shadows from the moonlight form a mesh of light over the stuffed chairs, and the moonlight dissolves the bookcase into a massive painting: no title, no book, no writer, no time, only the moment.

It comes to him that he is the Shadow, a shadow of some kind; and that it is he who must do things that others are not doing, and to be hidden like a shadow. The image of Mary Ann given a drug, and the woman who died with heroin as her partner, rolled into Johnny's consciousness.

And then he spoke to himself without reflection, without thinking: That is the first thing I will do: I will find out about heroin. I will find out about love. I will protect Mary Ann. Seventy-five or a hundred years from now people will be different. There will be no heartbreak from drugs. Our people must be at the beginnings of all this, and Mary Ann is just my age. He held himself still and thought: I will be the Shadow.

Johnny lifts the window and jumps out. Reaching over his shoulder, almost as an afterthought, he closes the window gently with one hand, and in moments he is at a dead run down the steep hill, down Shelby Street, seeking nothing, at ease in the dangerous run, dancing through the rocks and the ruts where a fall at that high speed could mean death, down the hill as no one else in the town could, as he had practiced the run many times, as no one else would ever practice.

*To be continued...*

## Romance is Generous

Romance is generous. It is giving. True love touches in the field of space. The force of the universe is the knowledge and the sail, romance, the bloom. All the invisible flowers are as beautiful as wild roses, as beautiful as horses dancing on a moonlit field. As beautiful as a sunrise, indigo and apple green. A poem that honors love is a gift of love, like a flower; or, a key for the inward journey. And yet, to be a poet, one need not write a poem, but to live poetically: to live in courtship with spirit as it reveals the romance of being. Poetry without a poem lives in the heart as love, travels out on thought, and its words and deeds have no necessity of being organized.

# Hawks

Our family calls the road leading into Scotland Farm "The Avenue", though it is a country lane of straight stretches and curves lined in trees, many damaged and left after storms to grow in mysterious shapes, and open spaces of grass and sunlight, and the road runs as you travel it a half mile from the high cut through the rock at the highway into the shade of the passageway made from those cuts in the limestone cliffs – and the small over-reaching trees envelop it as you move – and then sailing from the sun dappled tunnel away a half a mile to the tall, wide, brick house on the hill. The avenue is lined and scattered with trees, unpruned. The tallest are black walnut and wild cherry, and now and then there are groves and lines of them in the fencerows. There are locust and oak, too, and others, old and scattered.

The tremendous oak, one hundred and fifty years old, now lies on its side, a home for the rabbits and snakes and wandering chickadees. The trees are bare in winter, and even in summer the way the branches hang and the dead ones jutting out with no leaves but still strong, and anyone walking or driving there might see a hawk on a branch or hawk flying; and another big red-tailed hawk, his mate, will be nearby; and maybe she will be flying soon.

This pair of the hawks, just the two, live and hunt that ground, year after year. It is said that the red-tailed hawk is the only hawk that mates for life, and that their voice stands out from all the rest in that world, carrying a strength of being in the sound, greater than any raptor.

If you want to be like the hawks – which is a strange thing to want to be – that is, like the red-tails that live on my avenue, there are certain requirements, certain aspects of your character that must be changed, deeply and in fact. The first is that you will never complain.

*The hawk never complains.* She may describe a distorted situation in action, even in voice, but never complain about it. Appropriate to the time, the hawks deal with it. When I come rolling in or sailing by in my car and one of the hawks is near the road, in perfect position to take a mouse he has seen peep from its burrow, and I interrupt, there is no complaint.

With just enough awareness for safety from me, the unpredictable man, when my car comes close the hawk simply flies out and banks in behind me and takes up the old position with an easy disregard. Could you do it, if as they say, your dinner – meaning anything connected to your strong expectations – was rudely delayed? Expectations? The hawk freed himself of those when he left the nest and learned to fly.

*The hawk receives scattered inputs, moves them around, then, with timing, at the right moment, acts.* If I am walking down the long avenue, maybe even strolling, maybe with a friend, and maybe I am walking in the soft grass in the center of the long meadow against the road, the hawk might be there, settled in as before, and will begin flying a little ahead of me from one tree to a tree a few more down, landing and waiting; but I keep coming.

She wondered if I would turn around, and the safe distance she was keeping to rest would be her last move. Yet I keep coming, enjoying the sun and the light conversation with my friend, and finally she banks away on relaxed wings for better, less populated ground. In time, she understands, then she acts; she doesn't complain like the intellectual crow or the overly emotional blue jay.

*Our hawks are patient.* It is a work for us, you and I, to be patient on a hill or down among the trees in a forest. It is as if you are standing on a hillside or in an empty forest with your arms at your sides and a cold, light wind is lifting a leaf or two at your feet. You are feeling the wind across your face and your hands give a little at your sides in the wind. Maybe it is winter. To be in the depth of patience then, deep in the Quantum Field, a meditative attention you have worked for, when the mind busies itself with nothing. A field of the Field, one at your feet, the other clear through you making up everything.

In that patience, you notice the wind and the leaves when it lifts them and the spiritual force of wind and your breath in your being, and the world becomes tender around you and your body is fresh, almost not your own, and now and then the place you are standing opens up and you know by the impact of that opening, without thinking, that the universe is spirit-filled and great and that you are fortunate to live in such a fine universe. It is there you can, without force, receive from your past intentions, and receive the gifts of the universe for which you have asked in that way. Our hawk sits on the empty limb. She is content, a guest of spirit. Satisfied and coded by the fine energy of the universe; she is pressed by nothing. She rests and hunts and loves in her animal way. Yet, we have an extra level, sometimes called consciousness, with which we can make a journey of completeness, an awareness forever.

*Do the red tail hawks on our avenue respond to us in the quantum field?* Maybe to say: *in the encompassing force that makes and moves the quantum field.* Now and then a hawk swoops in. Maybe you are driving the car and you are in a good place because you have been patient in a cool wind and your mind is not busy and maybe there is a friend riding with you, who is also in a recondite energy within and at ease, and the density of the worldly life has receded out of the body because of an expanded intention you have been expressing with the force of being; and a hawk, for no real reason, comes swooping in and lifts away. In our life, do we respond intuitively in the quantum field; do we refine that place in our spiritual heart? Is that shift beyond words into knowledge a truth to be explored? Do hawks swoop in on the unifying force? Can we, you and I, earn the force where the intuitive lives and sail beyond those animal wings?

*The hawk is not pushed away from what is rightfully hers.* Coming around the curve in the road walking toward the barnyard I saw the hawk high on a limb in the walnut tree, almost above my head. Something was not as usual with that hawk. A hawk would never stay in a tree close like that; a hawk would have seen me and flown before I was near. She just stood on the high branch dead still. It was then I saw the big, red fox squirrel. They give the squirrel the fox name because it is unusually large compared to the gray squirrel and its coat of fur is reddish in color, though muted compared to the coat of a red fox.

The squirrel was heavy and long and laid out straight and newly killed at the edge of the gravel and its fur had a wide streak of bright wet blood; it was bright, new blood on muted red fur. The hawk must have flown up to the tree when I was coming down through the yard. And yet something was still puzzling me. If the hawk was waiting to claim the squirrel she had killed, she was waiting in the face of a human being, in the face of a danger she would not ordinarily chance. Did she believe I was unable to harm? Overlooking the danger from man is a false judgment; was she too greedy for her prey for care? And yet, it was a true judgment – for I would not harm her – and did somehow the hawk "know" it, having seen me often over the years?

I had left the farm truck in the barnyard with a friend helping me there. We finished a few things and drove back toward the yard. The big hawk was standing on the ground by the dead squirrel right against the road. We drove up beside her and she did not move, but stared at me in the truck. I leaned my head out the window and looked down at the hawk, and she did not move. My eyes were only six feet from her eyes. I held there, meeting her dispassionate eyes and spoke to my friend in the truck, yet the hawk was immobile staring with those piercing hawk's eyes, nothing moving, wings at her sides, staring at me, waiting, fearless, protecting her kill – what was hers. We drove on to let her be.

A little later, walking, I curved around to the barnyard by way of the flower garden, where the white Narcissus were everywhere in bloom, and came back on the same road where the hawk had been, just to see. The hawk was with the dead squirrel across the road from where she had been and into the meadow on the ground only about 30 feet away. Too heavy to carry on the wing she was taking the squirrel in her beak and swinging her head and body tossing him about three feet each time, farther and farther from the road, where she could have her dinner in peace and safety. Maybe she would cut him up as she ate and fly the pieces to a tree. She was working hard, and she was still accepting my presence; I was only

30 feet from her. It would be natural for her to fly away and come back when I was gone. Maybe she accepted me because she could sense something less threatening. And, of course, she had watched me in the car and watched me walking in the fields over many years. *Or maybe the hawk's unrelenting tendencies for food made her take this chance.*

Hawks! We are human beings, not hawks. We can do good deeds. And we can do good deeds in a consciousness to rise, while on earth, toward the force of spirit that moves the universe. Maybe we will use that human gift – and not be merely a hawk resting in a tree – to move in different rhythms?

*And red tailed hawks mate for life.* We are not hawks, but we could give that mating for a lifetime a try, even if before we have failed it. We could give it a try beginning at any moment in time. The past is not our real business; it is the present moment in which we love, in which we live. For all things, the seeker lives with focus and thought in the intuitive sense she has cultivated – always from a fresh beginning in the moment – carrying with her, in her divine beginning, all with which she was born and all she has truly earned.

*And hawks make love high in the air* and fall together for distances like falling stars and then catch themselves on the wing, and maybe – it is lovely to think – they are enjoying in their careless fall, the bright, romantic air of springtime.

# Your Beauty

Your beauty
Is of the
Falling stars
In summer.
Lying under those stars,
In absolute closeness,
The universe
Finds its center
There in us,
At ease
Among all the galaxies.

## Harp Pike Snow

The universe has its center where we work for it, and play for it. The moon in Kentucky, right here, the moon. I remember the big snow out in the Harp Pike hills when I lived there. The snow was deep and freshly fallen and I was driving an old car with a trunk full of Osage Orange logs for weight and the snow was not falling anymore and nothing but the trees lifted out of it on the long ridge looking straight out over the many valleys; sea waves of snow in the full moon rather than hills.

And there was not a car in the slow driving the thirteen miles out U.S. 421 from Frankfort; and when I turned in on Harp, I saw in the old, small wooden houses, looking smaller covered with the snow, maybe five in three miles, the farming people at rest near an electric light or two.

I passed the gravel road that would take me back another long ridge to where I lived, a mile back, at the end of an ancient wagon road with huge stones making the bed of the road. I passed that road so that I could see the snow out the long ridge. The edges of the road had disappeared in the deep snow, and yet, I knew the edges where they had always been, edges that would disappear in a future that was not my business, a future as if nothing in this night of the full moon and the snow.

Everywhere with the moon it was as if a strange and tender daylight. It was just after nightfall and the moon was rising tremendous and clear and as tall as the fantastic barn that slides on by, and the moon made a soft daylight that was impossible to think of, but only to love in; because of the moonlight I could see everything. I was alone and the great spaces of cold were a sign of the world's emptiness, of the strict nothingness of form and color without the individual human spirit to be enhanced and made strong, to give the universe a center. The mountain people of that evening there in the snow-covered houses have all passed on. That truth is like the snow. And only love was my business then, and every night only love, even away from the lonesome ridge top with no other place to go, and the snow covering everything. Though alone, maybe a love one, alive somewhere out of time. I was alone in the white hills, driving, and she was warm and protected, surrounding me with love this night, and in a distant future.

# The Victorious Horseman

The restaurant reminded him of a train at night. It spoke of a high-flying plane. When you hear the plane and the stars are out, it is the same kind of night in which you would hear the fine whistling of a mystical train. Someday, he thought, I will be on that train.

Kate dug her nails into Johnny's forearm. Under her breath, she said, "Just keep your eyes off that woman, and every other."

The woman with the almond eyes was with her family. They filed through the high wooden doors. She wrote her name in an antique, leather book, and they waited their turn.

Jenny, who was five, with five, small ponytails, held on to the woman's sea green skirt. The woman happened to notice the nails sink into Johnny's arm. She noticed a steadiness in Johnny, and turned to her family.

Kate whispered as they waited for a table, still holding his arm, "I don't want to feel unsettled," she said. "We are breaking up…for me. I want to feel clear."

"It will work out," Johnny said.

"I don't think so," Kate said.

And yet, to most, it was any restaurant on any day. There was a woman at a counter making change. A waiter in a white apron with a long scar down his cheek was pushing tables together. He looked like a soldier or a fireman at work, someone focused when the payment was life. He had a clear, fearless gaze that he kept directed to his work.

Johnny and Kate were seated at a table for four

near the wall.

The family of seven, which included the woman with the almond eyes, was seated next to Johnny and Kate. The family was given a long table made up of three tables, which the waiter with the scar had pushed together.

Each table in the huge, white room had a white cloth and white napkins, and glasses that made a ringing sound when the children flicked their edges.

Joey, a boy of nine, tugged at his Mother's sleeve. "Listen, I think I remember it," he said. "He was born always laughing, and the world's madness went away. Aaww, I can't get it. What is it again?"

"He was born with a gift of laughter and a sense that the world was mad," the woman with the almond eyes said to Joey.

"Who was it about?" Joey asked her.

"His name is Scaramouch," she said, and she smiled at her son.

Johnny, whose back was to them and very near to their chairs, heard the words quoted from the book. He turned abruptly around and met the beautiful eyes of the mother. Her eyes were interested and kind; yet stress showing in her face told of another part of her being, a part universally accepted as life itself; and yet, Johnny had always believed it could be cleared away.

"Fine words," Johnny said to the woman. He knew the book by Sabatini. He remembered the beautiful line quoted by the mother with the almond eyes, not the politics of the book, if it had politics.

She smiled at Johnny, a smile of recognition Kate did not see, and turned again to the seating of her children at the long table. One child was a little girl of eight who could not hear and had never learned to speak.

Johnny smiled at little Joey, who was seated now, with his hands beside him on the chair. He smiled back shyly and stared at Johnny.

"Are you going to start talking to strangers again?" Kate said to Johnny. "You always talk to strangers."

"I'm sorry, Kate."

"We came here to talk to each other."

"I know," he said gently, a deep love and tenderness for Kate in his eyes.

Johnny was slender – strong from farm work in his youth. He had dark blonde hair swept back. His eyes were a clear blue, and he smiled with them easily. Kate was tall, lean, with blonde hair to her shoulders, green eye shadow, and tender, green eyes that seemed always to shift distant, as if she searched for peace on a high balcony.

Boris, the husband, the father of the family, was a professor of history. His eyes were languid behind elegant, tortoise shell glasses. And though a robust man, who might have been a football player, he held his fingers on the edge of the table for support as he stood. He told the children his shirt was burnt umber in color, so they would know the color's name, and on the shirt were finely wrought figures of skaters making small circles on a small pond in winter.

"Damn it to hell, everyone, if you don't sit down, we're going home," Boris said. The mute girl sat down as quickly and smoothly as liquid mercury and looked up at the monstrous bird.

They all looked to the penguin as if to a shooting star. It was a huge emperor penguin. The little deaf girl smiled up at it. It was sailing in a grand manner, suspended by wires directly above their table. Its small flippers were out like sails. Its head and body were tilted up a bit to give it loft. Designed, it had been a careful job, and its fake feathers were shinning as if it had been hung there yesterday.

"A penguin alone, strange for a gregarious lot, and flying too," the woman with the almond eyes said. She smiled playfully for the children. She touched the rim of her glass and scanned their faces. Her name was Olivia.

Though the restaurant was very long and full, with a hundred people talking, it receded into nothing for the family as they looked up at the lone, itinerant penguin.

The waiter with the scar was standing very near in his white apron, but no one noticed him. He was muscular, easy when he moved, not tall. He stood without impatience, as if he had more time than eternity could offer, and there was a sense in his calm demeanor that he had arrived at a distant station, and now he was going nowhere, as if he could rush no one who did not need to be rushed, ever.

"Sit down, all of you," croaked Boris, and he lost his balance as one of his fingers slipped from the edge of the table.

The deaf girl picked up her menu and stared at it, while the rest of the children slowly sat. Joey and his little sister, Jenny, the one who was five, took upward glances at the flying penguin. The little girl's hair was in five ponytails – she wanted one ponytail for each year – and she had a front tooth missing. She smiled at her brother mischievously, and winked. Joey smiled back.

"I know what I want," Joey said.

"Me too," said little Jenny.

"What?" Joey asked.

"I don't know," said little Jenny, and she burst into

wild laughter.

Johnny inched his chair a bit sideways so he could see some of the family at their table. They interested him, and especially so, since they had awakened in him that distant, youthful memory of Scaramouch, his gift of laughter, the madness of the world.

"Kate," he said quietly. "I want things to work."

"Then work at it," she said.

"I'm trying."

"You live in a dream."

"What dream?"

Johnny noticed the waiter with a scar stayed unusually close to their table. Though the restaurant was full and the other waiters were scurrying about, he seemed to be unhurried and unnaturally near.

"You always criticize," Kate said.

"I do?"

"You make fun of things."

"The trouble-causing things."

"You always bring up people's faults."

Johnny was quiet.

"You bring up everyone's faults but your own."

"Do I try at all with my own?"

"Try harder."

"I never make fun of you."

"I feel it, though."

The waiter with the scar brought a tall pitcher of water. He set it on the table between them, more slowly than seemed natural. Kate took a deep breath, waiting for him to withdraw.

"I want to have fun," Kate said. "I don't want to talk about life, I want to live it."

"What fun do you mean?"

"I want to go out and do things. You know that."

"It always involves drinking," Johnny said. "What about that?'

"Everybody drinks."

He was quiet. He knew she was not yet hooked, yet he knew well that she used alcohol for what it does in the system – and now and then, pills to calm her, to sleep. And there was his tragic sense that something in her had stopped dead still. Her habits were becoming a larger and larger portion of her awareness, sneaking in – not unlike the chemical habits of many of their friends. He felt a repetition that picked at her spirit.

"Everybody but you,' she said.

"I first quit to see what it was like to quit, as you know," he said. "I'll go anywhere with you, bars, parties, anywhere, if you just won't drink."

"Hell, Johnny, Jesus drank."

"Did he?" Johnny asked.

"I'll have wine with my lunch."

"They don't serve alcohol here."

"What kind of dive is this, some kind of halfway house for dead history and dead penguins?" She began to touch the sides of her water glass, and a tear rolled down her cheek. Quietly she said," I'm sorry. Forget it."

Boris, the professor, tapped his knife against the deaf girl's glass, and the girl watched the knife hit the glass: a crazed metronome marking the loss of time, a lizard snapping flies in the silence.

"Children, this is a historical place. Today you are going to learn something if you can sit still long enough. How about you, Joey, do you want to learn something?"

"Not really," said Joey, and he tightened his lips together.

"Well, maybe your sisters do. Why don't you think of someone but yourself all the time?" Boris adjusted his fine, shell glasses. He read, "This is the Thunder House, named by the family who has owned it the longest. They saw that lightning was focused here, that it often struck among the trees on this hill. They felt the strikes left something behind: an intuitive sense of life which carried them on. They considered themselves fortunate people, and lightning became a symbol of their ways.

"Look around you. The paintings hanging here are of people who have achieved something in their life. There is Daniel Boone, Simon Kenton, Mary Slaye, Ruth Williams, Bronston Jones, the black raconteur, Thomas Jefferson, the Indian chief Tecumseh. Go see if that is Tecumseh, Jamie."

In a starched, white dress, the twelve-year old walked stiffly between tables to the painting and spelled Tecumseh aloud from the brass plate.

"Right," Boris said. "That's the man. He was a leader, good fighter."

Johnny heard it all while sitting with Kate in silence. He knew a lot about the chief Tecumseh. He repeated inwardly then the words of Tecumseh, which he knew by heart: "I have made myself what I am."

Little Jenny brightened. "I like his shirt. Is that a feather?" she asked as she rubbed her spoon against her cheek.

Johnny wanted to say the words of Tecumseh aloud; he wanted the little boy, Joey, who was nine, to hear. Johnny had heard those words as a child and always remembered them. And yet, he felt refreshed in the thought that little Jenny was too young and happy to care.

The back of Joey's chair was near to Johnny's chair. The waiter with the scar had his back against the wall at Johnny's left shoulder. Johnny glanced at him briefly and wondered why he had nothing to do. Johnny then spoke to Kate loud enough so Joey would hear.

"Tecumseh said, 'I have made myself what I am.'"

"Damn it, Johnny," Kate said under her breath. "Whose table are you sitting at?"

The woman with the almond eyes could hear Kate clearly.

"You talk about communication," Kate continued in a harsh whisper. "And then you tell me something childish that you have told me before. Everyone knows we make choices. Give it up, Johnny."

Joey had heard Johnny clearly, as if a hand had been laid gently on his shoulder. He turned around in his chair.

"What did Tecumseh say?"

"He said, 'I have made myself what I am.'"

"What else?" asked Joey, resting his chin across the back of his chair.

"He said, 'I have made myself what I am, and would that the red people could be as great as the conceptions of my mind when I think of the great spirit who rules over all.'"

"What does that mean?" Joey asked.

Joey's mother put a loving hand on Joey's shoulder.

"Don't bother this lady and gentleman," she said. And yet she waited for Johnny's reply, for she had heard him from a place as deep as her own struggles, as deep as thought itself, and her almond eyes flashed to Johnny in recognition.

"That's okay," Johnny said and smiled at Joey. "Joey,

it means to do good in life, and learn what it is, and find happiness."

Joey was thinking, and he kept his eyes on Johnny. "How did you know my name?"

"I heard someone call you Joey," Johnny said. "I didn't mean to be listening, but we are sitting close here, and I heard your name."

"Thank you so much for your thoughts," Joey's mother said to Johnny, her eyes staying with Joey.

"I am sure we are all having trouble listening to each other," Kate said coldly. "Let's just move the tables together and make things easier for us all."

Boris and the children at the other end of the table went silent and looked up. The mute girl fixed Kate in her vision and lifted her little hands from the white cloth, as if she were playing a song in the air on an invisible piano.

"No, we are fine at our table," Johnny said. "You are having a family dinner."

"It was we who interrupted," the woman with the almond eyes objected. "But please join us. We would love to have you."

"Right," Kate said sharply. She was up in a moment, and with a grip on the two corners of the table, began to push it. The waiter with the scar stepped back and to the side with the ease of a bullfighter when Kate broke from her chair. Joey scurried aside with his heavy chair in tow as the two tables joined, the long one with the short one, making an L.

Both Johnny and the woman with the almond eyes noticed the waiter with the scar. Somehow his nearness took precedence in their attention over the joining of the tables. Each wondered that he was always so near, so quiet, when they did not need him.

The woman thought, He seems solitary and alone, and yet the feeling is that something of worth surrounds him, like summer.

Maybe he has seniority, Johnny thought, and he can just rest. Or maybe he is lame, but Johnny had seen him move fluidly, rhythmically, and knew he was neither sick nor lame.

Jenny, the little girl with the tooth missing, was now sitting across from Kate. She gave Kate a wink and a little smile, rather chirpy, as a little chickadee might seem to smile in spring. Kate quickly looked down at her hands and held back tears.

Everyone was introduced around the table, and then came a deeper silence, as if little tree frogs stopped their singing for the night.

Down the long, white room the wind was blowing through the high, cathedral windows, fluttering the yellow curtains. The yellow curtains lifted higher in the wind. Silence came over the room as the curtains lifted out.

Before the din of conversation again flooded the restaurant, Olivia spoke quietly to the children. "The curtains were dancing" she said. "Like spirit flowing through."

"What's spirit?" little Jenny asked. She put her tongue in the space where her tooth was missing.

The mother opened her golden eyes wide and leaned to the little girl and spoke to her about spirit.

Boris tapped on the deaf girl's glass. She was looking over her shoulder to see if the curtains would lift again, and she cared little for watching the knife on the glass.

Joey ignored his father. He continued to stir his ice water with a fork.

"What did Scaramouch do?" Joey asked Johnny.

"I don't remember," Johnny said. "But I'll bet he tried always to learn, and tried to do good for those around him. I'll bet he was very…."

Boris tapped again.

"It is not often you will dine in a place like this," he said, "surrounded by the portraits of so many daring and able people, to remind you of what can be done in life."

"Where are they?" little Jenny asked.

"They are in books," said Boris.

"Like the books at school?"

"Yes, like them."

Johnny faded inwardly, and he thought of the winds over the ruins at Uxmal. He thought of wet, green jungles and how they move like a terrapin. He thought of ruins all across the earth, and edifices protected from ruin. He thought of words, no longer fresh, handed down from other times as truth – from those lives blowing lonely over stones. Now is not the same as then, he thought. When I want strength to care for the time that I am in, my place, my people, I will remember briefly, the winds over the ruins at Uxmal.

Olivia put her hand out near Johnny's hand and nodded toward her husband at the head of the long, white table. Boris had spoken to Johnny, but Johnny didn't hear him speak.

When Olivia reached out, Kate pulled her hand away from where it had rested near Johnny's on the white cloth. That old feeling swept over Johnny that he could not help her, that he could not soothe her, that he could not give Kate ease.

"You were drifting," Boris said, with lifted eyebrows.

"He always drifts," Kate said. "Don't you, Johnny. Don't mind him; he always drifts." Her eyes shifted from

Boris to Johnny and back to her hands.

"What do you think of history, sir," Boris asked.

"Seems important for learning about humanity, culture, ourselves," Johnny said. "It is a good story if not twisted too much, or used as a tool of control." He spoke warmly to Boris. "The right amount at the right time, in the right way, you know. Seems we are evolving and need history to help with our thinking."

The waiter with the scar had somehow appeared and was standing not far behind Olivia. A breeze lifted, and an odor of trillium swept through the great dining hall. It was an odor that rolled in like honeysuckle with a restless edge.

"I like history all the time," Boris said. "Know history; know thyself."

"Well…," Johnny began.

"History is like a rock to lean against," Boris continued. "Like a big, fat, friendly rock."

"Rock on," piped up Joey.

"Shut up, Joey," Boris said. "You're not funny. Take that fork out of your ear."

Olivia felt the presence at her left shoulder. The waiter with the scar was looking a little downward and to the right, as if he might be resting. She looked at Johnny. Johnny was watching Kate, searching for a way to make it all better, her life itself, easier for her.

"Is the penguin history?" asked little Jenny.

Johnny smiled at Jenny, who was looking from person to person for an answer. He then glanced casually toward Olivia, who had just put her hand on the shoulder of her daughter in the white dress. Kate saw the glance and squeezed his forearm to warn him.

The mute girl's eyes wandered like moons to the

waiter with the scar and fixed there, as if to rest in him, as if he were a quiet, night sky.

The penguin swayed on its wires in the same breeze that brought in the trillium – a breeze that gave an inward sense to the group – a sweet breeze, with a restless inclination toward peace.

"No, the penguin is not history." Boris was piqued. "Unless you study the history of penguins. But that is actually the study of birds, ornithology."

"I'd like to study birds," said little Jenny with a huge smile. "What's its name?"

"It's a penguin," Boris said, trying very hard to drop the subject. "That's as far as we can go today, unless, of course, someone here is a penguin expert. No?"

"Its name is Sally," chimed the twelve-year old sitting at Boris' left. Boris slapped a hand to his forehead in frustration, but with bad aim knocked his glasses askew, then slumped in his chair.

"I think its name is Herman," said little Jenny.

The deaf girl smiled and spread her arms out toward the penguin, and as she brought them down, her glass of ginger ale hit the floor, shattered and spread. The man with the scar seemed to be there, almost as it happened, and he wiped it up and gathered the glass in a soft towel. It was hardly noticed.

"Okay, Dad," Joey said, picking up on his father's frustration and wanting to fight the war that he felt raging between them. "What is the penguin's name?"

"Its name is Hey Penguin," Boris said wearily, and then suddenly he felt surprise at his own humor and burst into laughter; and everyone at the table laughed with him.

"Mom?" Joey asked.

"Her name is Love," Olivia said. "See how her arms are outstretched."

"She's flying," the child in the white dress, said in an offhand way.

"She's Herman," little Jenny said. "No, I want to go again. She's not Herman, she's Sweet Pancake." She folded her arms across her chest with a bounce, as if she had settled the issue.

"How about you, Mr. Tallifer?" Olivia asked. She felt it was time to lose her fear of Kate.

"Johnny."

"Yes. Johnny. Thank you. What would you name the penguin?"

"I think Scaramouch with all his laughter."

"Me too," said Joey. "I think Scaramouch, too."

"Kate?" Johnny said, and turned to her with a smile.

Tears were already on her cheeks, and she bowed her head slowly down. Then she looked up, and by some chance her eyes met Joey's eyes, wide with wonder at her crying. She turned in her chair and walked quickly from the room, holding her hands close to her sides.

Johnny stood and tipped his water glass with the back of his hand. He caught the glass in mid air as it left the tabletop and the water splashed to the floor.

As he looked up, there was the mute girl smiling directly at him – for him – a blazing smile, her beautiful white teeth and deep silence sparkling with joy. She saw that he too had spilled his water, and she saw that he did not care.

In the little girl's smile, Johnny remembered a woman, Jean Harlow, a star from long ago, laughing in a silent film. She was whirling and dancing about a simple room. Her blonde hair was white in the studio lights, her skin pale. The black shadows from the lights kept her on earth. He remembered another girl, Kate, still beside him, bright with free laughter before she took on the edging of the world. He saw hope in Jean Harlow's smile and hope in Kate's, and now he saw it again.

The man with the scar was there in a heartbeat. He had a wide, white cloth. He laid it gently in the water on the table, and deftly wiped the water from the floor, as he had for the deaf girl. They all watched him as they might a watchmaker drop in a tiny wheel.

As the waiter stood up, Boris spoke to him. "If you don't mind, if the owner is here, we would like to know more about the history of this place."

"I am the owner," the man with the scar said quietly. He stepped back a few steps as if he was positioning himself at the right distance from the table, a distance only he understood: not too close, not too far away.

"Oh," said Boris, taken aback. "Well, I want to ask. Do you have a trunk in your attic which has papers on your home, the history, the land, your family, its art?"

Kate came back toward the table and stood at the right hand of the owner with the scar. She could not get past him between the wall and the table. Johnny saw the owner's awareness of Kate, but the owner did not move or acknowledge her. He blocked her way pretending he did not know she was there. The owner wanted to keep Kate standing beside him, Johnny realized, to keep her near, so she would listen in closeness.

When he spoke, his voice was musical, strong. Everyone, suddenly, on hearing his voice, cared for him. Even the children did not lose their concentration; they watched him. His gaze was easy and direct. He was no longer something vague. He filled all the space between them.

"Thunder House, this mansion, this home," he began, "was built a long time ago, by a restless man, restless rather like some of you. Maybe the days were very hot. Maybe someone carried water to the workers from the well. If they worked late, they looked up at the evening star. They had their thoughts of love and work and eternity. They did not know that the house was not real, but only a brief whisper, mist across the fields. They thought the brick was a brick, maybe even forever. They looked up and saw what they had built but did not know that it was not there. They were gathered around a vision. The vision was of a future that never came, and the house was a deft mirage. Many people gathered around that mirage. They ate and drank and told jokes and had a fine time, and none of it was there. They married and had children who were not there. The children took off running as mist. The home was built in the year of the empty time, waiting to be filled….

"There is an ancient trunk hidden away here at Thunder House. It is in the penguin, or the yellow curtains as they lift, and the wind, and you could imagine it in those places. It is there to be opened. Inside is history, home, land, family. Yet there is something different about this dusty trunk, if you want it so, for inside is a pool…for you, a pool like the green sea with the sound of the surf gently whispering. If you are happy enough, easy enough, enough full of play, you will dive and swim and pass by and see and handle all history, all home, all land, all family, and by and by, you will have observed it all, played with it all, experienced it all – not with the close-set eyes of the scholar, but with the swift glance, the rolling understanding of the heart. That swim brings freshness and perception and a sense of all that is there in what is not there. You find yourself in the attic of the house that is not there, surrounded by the affection of the stars, by the love made of everything."

He stood for a moment. No one spoke. He smiled. "May I bring you dessert?"

Kate was leaning against the wall beside him with her eyes closed. She slowly rolled her back off the wall, quietly left the restaurant, and drove away. Boris stood and gathered some of the children, and took them home. The rest stayed. Before he left, Boris shook hands with the owner with the scar, thanked him for his hospitality and told him simply that the meal was good. Little Jenny, Joey and their mother with the almond eyes said they wanted to stay for dessert. Johnny stayed, too, though he watched the door for Kate. Nothing in them wanted to leave.

The afternoon opens slowly as afternoons do in the rolling meadowlands of Kentucky. The rest of the diners have gone; the great, white room is quiet. The man with the scar brings them tea and small, tasty things to eat with their tea. Sometimes he sits and chats with them about nothing in particular.

Little Jenny asks him what it is on his cheek. He tells her gently that it is a scar, and that in living life sometimes scars happen, but they can heal, and that he got his when he was taking a journey on horseback and "ran into a limb of a mimosa tree, or could it be a flowering cherry, a crooked one… you know, the one with the pink blossoms."

As the afternoon softens and stretches out, Kate walks in. She looks pale. She moves easily across the room as if she lives there in that room and has no other place worth going to.

There is an extra chair. Kate stands beside it and smiles in kindness to Jenny and Joey, and the woman with the almond eyes – to everyone at the round, white table where now they sit by the window with yellow curtains and trillium banking in on the breeze. She looks at Johnny and bites her lip.

She speaks, knowing everyone will listen. "I want to change, Johnny. I like your people. I like you. There is no place really to go in life. Every place seemed a mirror of the next as I drove away, though not here, not here on a day like this with you. And I will not be as I am. Those parts of me I saw today, I don't like them. What good is independence without a clearing of the soul. Why would I trade your friendship away, even though I feel pushed by you further than I can stand? And if I am able to become new, well, there I'll be; I can discover then some of the little things and the greater things about love."

Johnny lifted her hand and tenderly held it against his shoulder. Kate saw the man with the scar talking by the kitchen door.

"He is still here," she said. "What was he saying to us?"

"He was telling us about himself, I think. It seems he was offering what he knows."

"And?" Kate asked. She held tightly to Johnny's hand.

"Maybe he is Scaramouch," Johnny said, "and Tecumseh and Mary Slaye. Maybe he is Bronston Jones and Ruth Williams. He is what we could become. He has been what we are. He is all of those people as they might have lived in the unseen; he is what they were and what they could have been. The cashier told me he seems smart like a teacher or something. She said maybe he studied like a teacher. 'We can't figure him,' she told me. 'But if he teaches life, or something, it's not my thing. I know life. You can't be as untroubled as he is and know life.'"

The woman with the almond eyes is listening to Johnny. She is thinking. She has her hand on Joey's shoulder. "It is a state of being," she says to them. And her eyes are flashing. Her voice is brilliant, soothing. They all turn to her and hold there, as if to a center toward which all must turn.

The man with the scar walks up quietly; he looks easily about for a table to clean, a chair to straighten.

Kate smiles at him in a simple hello. He nods with a hint of a smile, and he looks down intently and moves a chair a bit to the right.

"Johnny says that you are a little different person than we are accustomed to, " Kate says. "What is it about you? Why did Johnny say that?"

He looks up brightly, as if in surprise. "I am your waiter, at your service." He laughs, and everyone laughs.

Little Jenny's five ponytails bounce like springs for her chance to talk. "Tell me again, how you hurt your face," she asks with a bright look of hope that he will answer her.

He pulls a chair in next to her and begins to speak tenderly: "She was a beautiful tree, and I was riding out on horseback… I wanted a blossom to carry with me… it was spring… it was a flowering cherry. Or was it a mimosa? Does it matter? You remember, the one with the pink blossoms…"

## Your Garden

Be in that garden in springtime with the wind. There, in our secret garden, we live in rhythm, in the tender breeze, in the metaphysical shift from the senses to the spirit. Search, if we will, for a garden such as this one, and if we wish, hold it in the heart as truth. Lean near to it in singing or dancing or doing, and there comes a wave of love in the expansion of the soul, and we are near. We could rest in its leaves without poetry, with no words between.

This garden of flowers is deep and delightful, the infinite standing tall and welcoming – as waves roll in – waves of peace in Kentucky.

# Popeye Letter

Thursday, October 1, 2015

From: Popeye, the Sailor Man
Traveling at the moment

Dear John,

Good to hear from you as always.

We have talked about the inner world of Omar Khayyam, haven't we? Not Omar's environment. It is recorded that Mark Twain carried a certain quatrain of Omar's on his person every day of his adult life. He collected all the publications of Omar's *Rubaiyyat* that he could find; and Omar's quatrains were broadly popular in Twain's time. Twain even composed his own poetic quatrains in the manner of Omar. What did Mark Twain see there? We can reflect on Twain's journey.

Twain would have enjoyed and understood Robert Graves' later rendition into English verse of Omar's *Rubaiyyat*. Twain would have appreciated the strength and beauty there, and the knowledge of the symbolic use of "wine" (maybe Twain understood), as opposed to the hedonistic use of wine: get drunk, you will be dead soon.

But I am drifting pleasantly. I am supposed to talk about me, Popeye. You brought up the thought of who Popeye is and who he is not. Well, back to Omar. The other day I was looking around to see what was about, and I picked up a copy of a book, by some character named Idries Shah, in the chiropractor's office waiting room. I was just in for a routine checkup requested of me by Olive

Oyl. I am never hurting unless my creator drew me hurting after one of Bluto's left hooks. I was most recently, but not essentially, born a cartoon. You have helped me escape the frames again. Thank you, John.

Well, Robert wrote an interesting Introduction to Idries Shah's book, which book included an entire chapter on Omar and Rumi and Sir Richard Burton, the explorer; Sir Richard under the heading: The Higher Law – a bunch of those characters. A lot of the book was aimed at ruffling up those closed-down and bound in the minutia of the intellect. I was happy that other poor souls, who had to wait for the doctor and didn't want to read magazines, would have another choice. I went to the local Goodwill and found a number of books by this writer, all owned I noticed by a determined lady named Sally Miller; she had highlighted often and intelligently. I assume her estate donated them. I opened one to this quatrain by Omar Khayyam:

> If from wine am acting like a drunk, I am
> and if I am an infidel and idolator, I am:
> Everyone's got a theory about me –
> But I am mine, and what I am, I am.

Was I surprised? Not at all surprised. So now you know what I mean when I, Popeye, sing out:

"I am what I am and that's all I am."

It is what I have become.

Love to you and yours,
*Popeye the Sailor Man*

Olive sends love as always. She just got home from town and is laughing about something. I am not surprised. We find humor everywhere.

And this too, the mystical understanding seems to be contained in a question and an answer: 'Who am I?' Answer: 'I am here.'

It is beginning here, in the moment we are in, and never-ending, here, in our moment enhanced.

Seems that the scholars and historians who write books about it and are quoted on the web, in general, don't know it; it is of itself, and existed always. It works among us and is of our original essence: peace and love, if you will.

Let's get together some friends and have supper soon.

Love Abides, Popeye

# We Dance

We dance,
A tune
Made for us,
Dropped in
From the Field's
Light-filled song,
Caught in arms
Opened by our striving.
We offer an empty page
To love,
On this page the music is written,
Love leads from space,
We dance—

# Chicago Memories

I think of being alone as a small boy, at eight years old and after, in Chicago at the Art Institute and the Field Museum and walking there through the crowded Loop on a weekday, to Marshall Fields, too, or to the little second floor, one-room boot store on Randolph Street where I bought my boots for the farm, and how strong and firm the boots were and what strength and ease they would give me in the snow and mud of the country; or alone in a taxi with a stranger driving, usually silent, driving me somewhere; or the first time I knew that there was such a thing as a southern accent, or any recognition of accents at all, when the teenage girls who were ticket-takers at the Field Museum laughed at my accent playfully, "You all open right now?" "Yes, we all open.", the tall one said in her best rendition of me.

I remember the very quiet downtown streets at night when my father and I would walk out to buy a paper at the corner news stand, and the Italian man so glad to see Mr. Hay, yet formal, and talking with my father, and both were quiet and respectful and warm. And to stroll on down under the skyscrapers and peek through the peep holes to watch the skyscrapers, illuminated by floodlights, being built around the clock, and later stopping before the three-story Picasso sculpture which we both "liked" in some undefined, silent way. We would stand before it, look upward three stories and breathe. Quiet, my father and I, relaxed.

And alone in the Art Institute I remember the paintings of Matisse, Picasso, and those others, paintings as if painted by aberrant angels, and the huge world of feeling of life they represented; and the caveman exhibits at the Field Museum behind glass, and the dinosaur bones they put back together, huge and only mildly interesting; and the people on the sidewalks, on their way, intently, men in ties or work clothes, and many women in high heels, and the extravagant feeling of the counters and the clothes at Marshall Fields, which I did not care to buy, nor have such money to buy; and the men and women who helped you, dressed up fashionably themselves, and leaning down to me to speak, and the smell of their perfumes and cologne and the powder on their faces, and the genuine smiles, and the implications to a country child of the mystery of their private lives somewhere else.

I remember the hotel, the Union League Club, my father managed, and his meditative touch through all the halls and pathways which he was responsible for as manager of the hotel, and the caring in his eyes for some of the art collected there, when he would stop and breathe for long moments before a fine painting he had looked at for years. A powerful man, I remember his extremely gentle nature there, and his sensitivity to my small and youthful presence. I remember my mother there letting go the demands of farm life in Kentucky, and dressing for the evening meal, and appreciating the meals prepared for her in the three-story dining room with the walls hung with paintings: each painting with its light; and the cathedral windows – her gentleness, too, her farm life, and her sensitivities to all the different internal lives she must pass through, hopeful and vigilant.

I remember waking up alone in my room in the hotel, the room reserved just for my short visit, a room opening into my father's apartment, simple and unadorned, with white crisp sheets – nothing to engage me but myself and the memories in my short life – aware of the tremendous aloneness, just there in the little room with nothing familiar about, in a strange country, with parents who loved life, and yet, introspective, always looking into the unknown and brushing at the mosquitoes of the known; purifying their thought, finding deeper pathways of love, with only love to help them court a deep knowledge of that shining internal country; just love for help.

# Yaqui About the House

When there were revolutions, one after the other, in the old days in Mexico, whoever had the Yaqui Indians fighting for their side always won. The Yaquis were fierce fighters, incomparable trackers, able to go on with little food and water, and patient when the necessities of time stretched before them and they had to wait. This was all true, because of some extra element, indescribable, that was in them; some connection developed in them over time, and individually, a connection of strength in the rhythms of the natural world. They found ways to use that strength, and maybe they sensed its eternal nature, as something made them a great force as far as was true and practical for what they found themselves faced with on earth; and, in a higher, unending sense, maybe fearless.

When my father was a young man starting work in a hotel in San Diego, a man would come to the hotel, a distinguished man, who was a vice-president of Standard Oil. He looked like an Indian from Mexico, at a time when these people were not highly considered in California. My father didn't ask his origins. The man was polished and spoke elegant English, and Spanish, and strangely, Yaqui, too. He would rent a room, leave his fine clothes in the room and put on the rough clothes of an Indian peasant and disappear into Mexico, into Yaqui country for a month or more at a time. My father was taken by him and would talk to him and ask him questions to discern his intentions. When my father would describe him to me, or repeat his words, you could feel that it was a gentle strength, a great kindness, an inner force he felt from this man.

The man told my father, at that time – (and my father knew of Yaqui country being closed) – that one of the Mexican politicians years before, in order to stop the use of the Yaquis to win revolutions, devised a plan to drown them all in the sea a few at a time, telling them they were getting new rich land, showing such land to a few of them, and taking them, a small number at a time, and drowning them. One Yaqui escaped by swimming a tremendous distance to shore, made the long journey home, and warned the rest. From this time, Yaqui country was closed. Not even armed commands of Mexican soldiers could survive a foray into Yaqui country. But there were two outsiders who could enter, this man told my father – those two were an old man who traded gold with them, and himself, our polished gentleman who leaves his clothes in a hotel room and vanishes into the desert. "Why do you go?", my father asked him. The man only smiled mysteriously and said, "I like their ways". After a few of these meetings, when the gentleman would rent a room in the hotel and leave for Yaqui country, he and my father got to know each other. And one day, as my father asked further to learn more of his mysterious travels, the man said, "If I took you into Yaqui country, if we went in together, they would kill us both. But I could teach you things, certain things, so that you could enter their country on foot alone, and they would not kill you and you could stay with them and you could return. Would you be interested in that?". "No" my father said. "I don't wish to go." My father had a new job and a young wife, two young children – maybe that was his hesitation – and I could tell when he told the story that he had been, in his heart, tempted. He had felt something from this man, something fresh and clear and fearless; I could feel it as he told the story to me one fall day in the kitchen at Scotland Farm, our home, with the windows open and the soft breeze wafting through. He only told me the story, not so many years ago, in the middle seventies.

He told me the story only because of a coincidence that happened to me that day. I had been reading, Journey to Ixtland, a very unusual book, a modern book which claimed anthropological truth, (Truth which has been questioned), about an unusual Yaqui teacher, called in the books, Don Juan. A University of California graduate student in anthropology, named Castaneda, older than the usual graduate student, had met the man in Mexico and had written popular books about him. In a later book, *Tales of Power*, in which Carlos Castaneda carries his adventure forward, strangely my father's acquaintance from the hotel fits the descriptions of Castaneda's Yaqui teacher exactly, down to being a stockholder, being finely dressed or roughly dressed, educated in his speech, even the age of the man at the time my father would have known him. Could they be the same man? They do share radically unusual characteristics.

J. Frank Dobie, the writer from the University of Texas, also wrote an essay about a Yaqui he had known as a guide with the same unerring intent and strength, but nothing like Castaneda's eloquent teachers as described.

It is my view that Castaneda, early on, met this individual – one of the two – and carried on with his books in a literary and imaginative way, not as a rendition of actual happening.

That morning, looking for something else in the house, I opened a small, lower wooden door on a large glass-doored cabinet and saw a group of very old 78 record albums, the paper kind, that held a number of records. I pulled one out at random and it was a recording of Mexican Indian ceremonies done by researchers, maybe in the twenties or thirties. After playing it – I was taken by the calming and mystical impact of the Yaqui music, and the Yaqui coincidence. I went into lunch and told my father of the book I was reading, and the music, and he told me the story. I was cooking for us that day; my mother was out. I remember questioning him for more, and this was my father's story.

I remember wishing my father had taken the man up on his offer, learned what he had to do and be, and traveled into Yaqui country. Now I better realize that we all choose, and that I trust the intuition of the young man, my father, in the 1920s and the 1930s, just starting out, who was fortunate enough to meet a strong individual, to feel his peace and strength and kindness, and to carry his story, and much of his truth, with him in his heart and feelings. That was the mood of the conversation in the kitchen at Scotland Farm that fall.

# Indian Ponies

We rode hell bent for leather, my friends from town and my cousins from the farm next door. We rode strong, swift-running horses and we rode for the excitement and the peace of the horses and the rolling, green fields. My cousins had a bunch of horses. One was a half thoroughbred paint named Honey. A couple of the older boys were always on her. But I watched as she laid back her ears and flew across the fields, stretching out, sure of foot, never a stumble over dangerous ground: death dealing groundhog holes, steel-like branches of Osage orange, or the bleached white bones of a cow long dead. Honey could dip low on the run. She seemed to be at her most romantic on the run, in her graceful, heaving curves between the trees flashing by, through a gap in the fence, leading us to our next field of adventure.

We had bawdy names for all the gates and gaps we passed through, comic phrases, unrepeatable at home. We were inspired and secure at heart when hanging on to the mane of a horse at a dead run. Our horses sailed as swift as a pirate ship on the black and white celluloid sea with Captain Blood at the helm; we were as daring as Lord Johnnie.

We named them. There was Satan, for good reason, Honey, Pretty Thing, Blade, and Miss Minerva named by a little sister, but we kept the name anyway. There were paints, bays, chestnuts, buckskins, and Sport the big Appaloosa. They loved to run. Nothing in our lives was as fast as the horses we rode. We could imagine nothing faster. Cars didn't count; we weren't old enough to drive them, and cars were cold and heartless and had to stick to the roads—entirely boring.

Bareback always, we would take off at a nod. In a heartbeat, Satan and Pretty Thing would be side by side at a dead run, and my cousin Timmy, riding behind me, would jump from Satan to Pretty Thing and back, getting a hand from my cousin Edmund who was riding her. No one ever fell. We were Tecumseh and Chief Joseph. We were the Lone Ranger and Lash Larue. We were knight errants protecting beauty. The drum of the ground thumped under the hooves. Our focus and concentration were impeccable. The horses disregarded our daring; ears laid back, they took themselves for a run, the leather reins loose and swinging against their necks.

We would ride into the woods at full tilt and swing from the tree limbs letting the horse run out from under us. No bones were ever broken. And if we fell into walnuts with rotting shells, the walnut stain would ruin a shirt if we had one on, or give our skin battle marks that happily took weeks to wear away.

We liked to think of the Indians. When I was very small, my mother read Blackfoot teaching stories and myths to me at bedtime. That could be a pretty rough way to be led into sleep, as the stories often taught lessons in a rather fearful manner. Rascally, cantankerous, death-dealing "Old Man" was often the protagonist. Yet we liked the beautiful illustrations by Charles Russell and the romance when the Indian princess appeared. Chief War Eagle told the ancient stories of his tribe, lit by the flames of the open fire in his teepee on starry moonlit nights, passing them down to the young ones.

The farm was as quiet as a meadow at the beginnings of time. Birds would whistle, the wind would sing, a dog would bark near home or way far off, a crow would caw caw caw over the distant shine of snow in the eye of winter. Spring brought yellow flowers, chestnut foals, shaggy calves, and baby rabbits, which were brought down laughingly by angels. School and work on the farm after school were in the mix. We lived in the bluegrass, young and tied to nothing.

My father was unusual, at times spontaneous you might call it, a romantic toward animals. He liked donkeys, birds, horses, and cattle, wildlife, the outdoors, all of it. One day when he was away with his work in the city, he called long distance and said that some Indian ponies would be arriving soon.

"What is an Indian pony?" I asked.

"They are wild horses from the West," he said. "These are from Colorado. I saw an ad in the Chicago paper, that they were being gathered up on the range, and if someone would buy them they would be saved. They are all wild. I got them cheaply. The government is looking for homes for them. They are sending a truckload. They are descended from the horses of the tribes."

We had plenty of horses for breeding. I had a horse to ride. We had cattle, peacocks, chickens, ducks, dogs, and the problems and pleasures of caring for them. Yet these Indian ponies were for my father. The romance of horses and the Western plains was in his heart.

Indian ponies! They were a fresh mystery for me.

Before the truck arrived, something changed in me. It was a focus, I guess, reining me in, stopping me for a deeper look. I was to get my license to drive in a week or so. My friend Jimmy got his license early. After school, he would drive out to my farm in his parents' green Pontiac to catch the horses for a ride. Yet, a little older now, we rode the horses over the farm a lot slower, just looking around, talking about life, not letting the horses run free for one of those wild rides across the fields.

Jimmy liked to tell me about a younger girl named Sharon from another school, and how they liked to drive around at night, going nowhere in particular. Her mother didn't know. Then it wasn't long before Jimmy said he wouldn't have time to ride horses after school, as he was going to pick up Sharon.

Olivia, my true love, said that we must be apart, that she was leaving for a semester's credit at an archeological dig; and, in her way of speaking, often taking in the whole of things, she said that I should live as if she might never return. In some generous manner, Olivia was speaking of my freedom to learn, to be with people freely. Soon after, Lorraine left me a note. I hesitated to tell Jimmy about the note, but finally I did as he was talking so much about Sharon. Lorraine, a year older than I was, had left a note in my locker asking if I might like a ride home after school one day. I had not told her yes, and it had been two weeks since she had asked. I wish I hadn't said anything to Jimmy. "Are you crazy," he shouted? "She's more than cool. Every guy in town wants to go out with her. She just broke up with an idiot from college. Wake up. Olivia is gone; she is not thinking of you." And he kept going on and on like that about Lorraine. Jimmy knew of the mystifying closeness, for so many years, of Olivia and me. Our relationship was otherworldly to him; he didn't understand it. To Jimmy, Olivia and I traveled strangely from one arcane passageway to another, sometimes together, sometimes apart.

"What is this Olivia deal?" Jimmy would ask. "I

don't get her. I don't get you for that matter. I see you together and then I don't. You all act like some kind of guardian angels, not just plain old boy friend and girlfriend. Don't you ever fight?"

"I guess it is a kind of mystery, Jimmy, even to me."

"Sometimes I think you two are real," Jimmy said. "Sometimes I think you are just a thought worrying my brain."

"You got me, Jimmy, maybe we are both."

The Indian ponies just appeared. No one called to tell us they were coming. It was on a Sunday. I heard the big truck with wooden slats for racks come slowly up the avenue. I grabbed the phone and called Jimmy. "Hey, Jimmy, quick, the Indian ponies are here." My father was working in the city; my mother was in town getting supplies for the week; so it was up to me to get the horses settled.

It was a strange time for these Indian ponies to come, as I had been sitting alone reading in an old leather bound book that had always been on a table in the house somewhere, a book I had picked up but never opened. It was a collection of poems, put together because they were all about something deep in a person's psychology, or about the mysteries of the universe. It made me think about life, and I remember settling into it, and sort of forgetting where I was, and just going out into a feeling of the hugeness of life itself. In the past, I had thought of those mysteries – what life and love might be – but never so clearly. I was taken by a quatrain telling poetically of a man and woman having a picnic alone on a desert beneath a bough, and another that spoke of generosity and laughter and scattering that across the world as gold.

How happy I imagined them to be! The arrival of the Indian ponies jerked me out of my thoughtfulness, but it took the walk to the barn to really shake the poems loose.

Jimmy must have driven at top speed, as he got to the barn while I was still talking to the truck drivers. I thought the men who delivered Indian ponies would be really top notch horsemen, bringing in wild horses from the desert, but they weren't. They were just there to get the job done and leave, didn't know a thing about horses. There was a small paddock near the hay barn where we unloaded them onto a wooden ramp and into the field.

The horses spread out across the field, some running to the corners nervously and then across the field to another corner and back. There were twelve of them. None of them were actually ponies but the size of horses that you might see the Native American Indians ride in the movies. There was a mix of colors, and they were not all well proportioned. All of them were lean. There was a dark bay with white stockings and long legs, and a small boned chestnut, both gaunt from lack of food. Most of the horses pushed close against the fence and moved along it and broke out toward the center and crossed to another fence, looking for an avenue of escape. They were all fillies and mares, no stallion among them.

Strangely, there were two who stood in the center of the field. They didn't run with the rest. There was a beautiful white mare; she stood with her head held high and looked around, now and then glancing our way, unafraid. Behind the white mare, a buckskin mare with a black mane and tail shifted about nervously, looked into the distance and back at the white mare. The buckskin deferred to the white mare, watched her for direction. The buckskin was taller than the others. She shifted from side to side and neighed loudly, but she would not leave the calm, white mare.

We filled the water trough for them and moved away. I knew horses pretty well. It was clear the white and the buckskin had been handled, but how much?

"I think the white horse might be broken to ride," I said, "maybe the buckskin, too."

"How can we tell?" Jimmy asked.

"Let's get bridles and a bucket of feed."

The white horse knew what the bucket was. Her ears came forward to look at it. The buckskin stayed close by, moved around her, avoiding us. We walked the white mare into a corner, and I soon caught her, and I held her with my arms around her neck, and Jimmy slipped the reins over her head.

Jimmy held the reins, and I moved to her side.

"What are you going to do?" Jimmy was nervous. I was nervous, too, but I knew we could just jump away if things didn't go well. I told Jimmy to stand to the side and hold the reins. I put my hands on her back. I pushed down with my hands; I patted her back, and then I slapped it firmly. She was quiet. I jumped up with my chest against her side and slid back down. She didn't move. I jumped and laid myself across her back. My arms and head hung over her opposite side; again I slid back down. She was quiet. None of that seemed to bother her. "Here goes, Jimmy."

I was up. She was truly a beautiful mare, all white with a long, white mane, tail and forelock. I got her going, stopped her, turned her a few times. It was amazing; she was expertly broken to ride. How could a horse like that be among a group of cheap, wild horses from the West. It didn't make sense. It was as if she was rounded up by mistake. Maybe she had escaped from a ranch and had been running with wild horses. I couldn't figure it. She neck-reined. I could lay the rein softly against the side of her neck and she would turn on a dime.

Immediately, I thought a great deal of her; she felt like mine, and she seemed to care in some strange manner, to care for what she was doing, focused right there with the time she was in. I fancied that she liked me; she seemed to. I felt strength from her, something I had felt from other horses from time to time, but never like this, never so refined, nor as attentive, nor as settled into the action of the moment. I had been reading those deep poems in the old leather-bound book when the Indian horses arrived. I had seen the word "spirit" in a poem that made me shiver, stopped my mind from thinking. Riding her, something of the feeling of the poem, like a shiver, a tingle in the back of the neck, came over me again. I decided I would name her Spirit.

I rode Spirit while Jimmy walked, as we forced the buckskin into a corner. Soon Jimmy was up on her, which was another surprise about these supposedly wild, untouched horses. Both Jimmy and the buckskin were wild-eyed. The buckskin was what is called "green broke," meaning broken to let someone stay on but not well schooled in responding to the signals of the rider. It was lucky that Spirit was there for the buckskin to follow. There was nothing smooth about the buckskin. She had a ridge of bone prominent in her lean back and a back breaking trot and a drunken walk. Jimmy screamed profanities complaining of permanent damage.

"This wench is going to kill me," Jimmy screamed in pain. "She is a man hater, killing my dreams." And then he yelled louder. "But I like her." He did like her, and soon went to the barn for a saddle blanket that he strapped around her for a cushion. He would not stoop to use a saddle.

She was a tall and lean mare with a black mane and tail. Jimmy said she was as good looking as Sharon. He liked to ride her. He said he felt like an Indian in the desert. He didn't really care what damage the mare did to him, or how she felt about the situation, or if she would learn: no future, just ride.

"Let's name them," Jimmy said. "I'm calling the buckskin Babe. Come on, my baby. Or should I call her Sharon? What are you naming the white?"

I always liked Jimmy's bluster. He got us laughing.

"Spirit," I said.

"Boring," Jimmy said.

"You're probably right."

"Hey, why don't I come back later, and let's go riding tonight out on the road," Jimmy said. "We've never ridden out on that road."

"Let's ride now."

"I have to meet Sharon this afternoon. We're going to drive out to the river road spot." He winked and then closed his eyes as if he were enjoying something tasty. "Why don't you call Loraine and go somewhere. She's hot for you. Girls don't ask to drive you home for nothing."

"Come back later," I said. "We'll ride on the road."

The road was a four-lane interstate highway under construction. It was going across country east to west, right through our farm, passing a few hundred feet from our home. The dynamite shook the house. Workers had completed construction of two ends of the interstate and were now building the last section, joining the ends together right there in a big field in front of the house where we used to graze and ride our horses. Part of our farm was now on the other side of the road.

Night had fallen when Jimmy arrived, and there was no moon. We caught the horses. There was just enough starlight in a shifting cloud cover to let us find our way. We knew where the gates were and how to double back to get up on the roadway under construction. The roadway was graded with fill so that the roadbed sat high above the fields like a low bridge. The road had been graded flat, and the horses were walking on dirt that had been flattened out by the big machines. In the near dark, huge earth-moving machines, forty feet long with twelve-foot wheels, would suddenly loom next to us as giant shadows in the starlight. We rode the horses slowly. It was almost entirely dark. Spirit moved smoothly and Babe followed a half a length back. Jimmy and I were both a little nervous, so he started talking, but quietly. It was so silent out there.

"Hey, why don't you get with Lorraine. And remember that girl, Melissa? I saw the way she acted toward you that night at the dance. She is a hot ticket."

"Lorraine still goes with a guy in college," I said.

"They must have broken up."

"Yeah, maybe."

"There is no one who wouldn't want to spend a little time with Lorraine. Right? I mean, what about those legs?" Jimmy said.

"She runs track."

"Come on, get serious. It's time you got up close to someone like Lorraine. You're not getting any younger."

"Right."

"I mean, listen, Sharon is really good to me. She...."

"You ever like poetry?"

"Yeah, yeah, don't change the subject. There is plenty of poetry in English class."

"Hey, Lorraine is nice. Okay?" I said. "I don't know her very well. She's great looking, good smile, but can't a guy be in a different mood some days?"

"All right, all right, all right. What about poetry?"

"Not just poetry. Something different, something else going on in some of it."

Jimmy's voice seemed to be a little distant as his last "all right" faded. Clouds had come over the stars, and the night was pitch black. I couldn't see anything.

"I mean poetry which talks about our thoughts and what we are doing with them," I said. "There were these thoughts I saw. I was reading in this very old book...."

Jimmy said something way down below me that didn't fit. "We could double date," I thought I heard him say.

Then I realized I had very gradually been going up some sort of strange hill in the dark where I knew there was no hill. I had forgotten about the Indian horse I was riding. I had forgotten that she was making her way in the dark, too, and that she looked to me for her direction. We had only just met – the Indian pony and I. Suddenly, she was going straight up, as straight up as a horse could go and still walk. I had to hold on with my knees squeezed against her sides and my hands wrapped in her mane. I felt her picking her way upward through rubble as if on a mountainside after an avalanche.

"Whoa," I said softly and held back gently on the reins.

She was climbing a huge mass of waste, a black mountain of refuse, iron and rock and broken forms, and matting used to contain the casualties of dynamite, all pushed into a mountain by the tremendous dozers. It was so quiet and dark out there. She was steady under me; there was faith from both of us. I felt that shiver at the back of my neck, as if from the poem, as if from memory of life over the eons. She was an Indian pony, a white horse with a deep understanding of the moment. She loved me gently from the beginning, just off the truck from far away. She loved me because she was made of love, and because I was there. Her name was in the poem I read. Under me I could feel her steady hold on life. We ended our struggle with the ruin that would soon shore up the constant moan of a highway. In that silent moment, high on the mountain of waste, so much was understood. It was so quiet and dark out there. She never flinched; she never faltered. She would have climbed forever.

## Your Eyes, The Eyes of the Stones

Life is not a sluggish thing. There is something happening in it that is pure. To endure it is insane. To purify and find the secret there, one must know life a gift. In the garden, the fine and carefully tended garden, Hatim Jones reflected on these things as he waited for the milkmaid to come. She would come out in the dawn in a dress that liked to play with the morning breeze.

She carried milk for her father when she was a child, and now that she was grown and just out of the school of those who attain – one of the few chosen to work in the field of science trying to rediscover from clues what was destroyed one hundred thousand years before during what was then measured in time as the 21st Century – she still carried the milk. She never forgot the feeling that went with lending a hand, nor that her parents took care of her when she was small and now needed her when they were old. She respected them and discussed with them their interests. So in the mornings she helped with the milk, and in those times did her thinking or merely looked at the play of light or told jokes with those who rise early.

Hatim used to whisper to her over the wall when he was thirteen and she was fourteen, but taken to the Southern Lands he had only a vague memory of her beauty and her easy ways. Home for only a few days, he again watched her in the mornings as he had at thirteen, through a chink in the stone. At ease in the family garden, gathering his own thoughts from some years of travel, he had not spoken to her, only watched and felt the strength of her character revealed in the way she walked, the way she carried the pails of milk, and in the way she greeted the children and how they loved to go with her.

Early morning! Sunrise! Dawn! The birds and the sunlight were drawing the sparks to make the day and there she was again in her crimson dress. Hatim made his way around the fountain and slipped out of the gate to hide himself by the roses against the stone. And there was a breeze for her dress to play with.

A little whistle from Hatim and she stopped to look behind her down the empty street. Another whistle and Hatim peeked from behind the stone. For a moment she stared at him gathering her thoughts.

"Hatim," she exclaimed. "It's been so long."

Hatim stepped out smiling. "You remember me," he said.

"Of course I remember you. I've thought about you often over the years."

"And I of you," said Hatim, pleased. "But I can't remember your name."

"It's Tanya", she said. "And shame on you for not remembering. I think of you every time I pass this garden and the little chink in the stone you used to peek through."

"I've been peeking through it again. I have watched you every morning this week as you delivered the milk."

"Then shame on you again, Hatim Jones," she said, lowering her eyes, but as quickly smiling brightly again. Hatim recognized immediately that she was a woman who know the importance of joy.

"Come into the garden and talk for awhile," Hatim said. "Will the milk be late?"

"Not so late," Tanya said. "I'll come in for a moment."

"And then we'll deliver the milk together," said Hatim.

The garden, well thought out, planted and tended, drew them in and soothed them with the red flowers and the white ones and all the green – a gift of nature made tender by man – a gift from the final mystery, well received.

"Today, I could just rest and look at the sky," said Hatim. "But we have time for that. Tell me what you do now that you are grown and still beautiful." Her eyes sparkled at the word beautiful.

"You first," she said. "You are the host of this garden."

The desire to talk to someone had been building up in Hatim, the desire to talk of that which had lain heavy in his mind. He sat on the edge of the fountain without noticing she still stood, and furrowed his brow.

"Lately, my thoughts have been heavy and disturbed," said Hatim. "After my studies in engineering I was sent South to the rain forests to describe and map them for the government. But lately I have been making more poetry with my pen than maps. Not real poetry about one I may someday love, but sad words or thoughts about our world. There is something happening I don't understand." He hesitated and looked up into her eyes as if he unconsciously felt her reading his thoughts.

"Tell me," Tanya said gently.

"It is the rain forests," he said. "But I have heard the milkman's daughter is a scientist now. Please don't think me foolish. Yet I have come to believe that the cutting of those forests is a dangerous thing. There is something happening, something is going wrong with the weather, with nature herself."

Tanya sat down very close to him on the rim of the fountain as if in a few moments, intimacy had grown. Her own face had gone pale. She seemed to quiver. She touched his arm lightly with her fingers. They trembled.

"Please go on, tell me," she said. "Tell me what you feel."

"They call it 'cut and burn' and millions of acres of the rain forests disappear each year and often the earth with a little farming goes bad, and no trees replace the old. Where there was greenness and life, a living world, there is now bareness." Hatim hesitated and searched in her eyes. "But are you really interested?"

Against her paleness, Tanya's eyes seemed to lose their luster for a moment. Her head tilted at a strange angle as if she would faint.

"Are you all right?" Hatim said, and took her hand in his.

"Go on," she said as a flat command. "It's nothing, talk, tell me. Waste no time."

"It's just my feeling – the droughts, the dry winds, the rising temperature, the vanishing forests – I feel they are somehow connected."

At that Tanya stood up and turned her back on him, her head bowed.

"What is it?" Hatim asked. "Why does it disturb you so?"

She turned to him and pulled herself up straight and looked into his eyes, her composure now strong, contained, her height and the power in her body unnerving.

"Yesterday," she said, "I discovered oxygen."

It was in the "Science of Recovery" that she practiced, a researcher chosen for that life, the cream of the scientific community. From the destruction of the old world one hundred thousand years before, certain artifacts, words and formulas were left intact, but their connections with meaning, the understanding was gone. Like little gods of old, words like oxygen or expressions like $E=MC^2$ sat alone without force to make them live. Icons without even the bones of ritual to sustain them lay on the boards. Scientists like Tanya hovered over them, over these and other pieces lying fallow like a surreal stream.

There were the traditional scientists who built from the blocks already known, but the Recoverers were of a different breed; the connections they made could jump the gaps of time. Tanya was of that ilk.

"I'm going," she said. "Goodbye, Hatim. I'll come back when I can."

"But you can't leave me like this, without explaining."

She swept up the two pails of creamy, white milk and walked toward the garden gate, her crimson dress pushed between her legs by the wind. Hatim followed and caught her by the gate.

"I promised I'd deliver the milk with you." he said.

"I am going to the Institute where I work. There is no time for delay".

"Then I'll help you carry it."

Before Tanya could resist, Hatim took one pail of milk from her hand as she slid through the garden gate, her long stride carrying her down the dusty road under the cool trees.

"Oxygen, what is that?" Hatim demanded. His tone was now as strong as hers. He sensed something to be done.

"It is a substance, a waste product of green plants, trees if you will, like there in your rain forests. It is a substance in the air."

"Impossible," said Hatim. "Air is a substance unto itself."

"Tanya, Tanya," came the cries of some little children who were playing with sticks in the road. They got up to meet her.

"Later," she answered and they stopped in their tracks like dolls, empty for a moment, to miss having their beloved Tanya come to them.

"Oxygen is a substance in air," Tanya repeated as she turned the corner into the voices and color of the main bazaar. "It is what you breathe for life."

A street vendor in the crowd hawking his wares of copper plates and hand-woven rugs stepped out in their path. Like dancing, Tanya made a full turn swinging the pail of milk and was around him. Hatim was left behind and caught her just at the door to the Institute of Scientific Learning. She showed her card and Hatim was able to follow her in. They stopped before the elevator.

"I don't understand, what does oxygen have to do with all this?"

"It's not only oxygen, but it's also the sign $CO_2$. I don't know the original word for the "C", but I know now what it is and what it does."

"So what is it? There is something I said that started all this."

"The stairs. This thing will never come."

Up three flights, two steps at a time, and they entered a large empty waiting room with thick carpets, and there was tense, boney woman at a black desk.

"I need to see the Director immediately," Tanya said.

The tense woman stared uncomfortably at the pails of milk.

"I'm sure he can't be disturbed this early, Tanya. You know his rules."

"But I must see him," Tanya pleaded with a voice that made Hatim shiver.

"I'm sorry, Tanya," the woman said through her clenched teeth.

Tanya turned briskly to Hatim and handed him her pail of milk, "Hold this, please." She then walked past the woman and disappeared down a dark hall.

"Tanya," the woman jerked in her seat but did not look back.

Hatim missed Tanya as if some part of him so newly felt, an energy, had drifted away. He sat down with the pails of milk on the floor at his feet and waited. An hour passed. Now and then the woman would glance disapprovingly at Hatim and then at the milk. Hatim tired of thinking, tired of wondering, got a glint in his eye. Finally he could stand it no longer.

"Would you like a glass of warm milk?" he asked.

The tense woman shuddered at the thought and her cheeks curled as if she had just bitten into a green persimmon. For a few moments Hatim thought he would burst holding in his laughter, then voices came from the dark hall. A man in a white laboratory coat appeared with Tanya. They were arguing. He was narrow shouldered, solid.

"If you won't inform based on this information," Tanya was saying, "then I must take it upon myself to inform them today!"

"Now Tanya," the Director said. "There is no real hurry, papers need to be filed, reports written. Personally, I think a few years of research are needed to…."

"Nonsense," interrupted Tanya.

The man in the coat stiffened, his eyes narrowed, he looked at her dangerously. There was a moment when nothing happened and then he noticed Hatim.

"Who is this?"

"My friend, Hatim."

"Does he know the nature of our talk?"

"Not really."

"Not really. I see. Then my order as your superior is final. You will be quartered here at the Institute until I make a decision on how to proceed. Your friend must stay as well."

"The hell with you, Mr. Director," she said.

The Director went red, veins in his neck bulged.

"Call the guard," he said to the tense woman.

Tanya began to run for the stairway. Hatim followed, a little unnerved that he would have to face the guards of the Institute. In the rain forests he had been his own protection and an expert hunter, but he had never trained to confront men. There were no real armies, no war in recorded history, but it was rumored that the kings, the benevolent rulers of the countries of the world – each country had one – were beginning to take an interest in weaponry, their interest in all cases initiated by their advisors. It seemed that some countries, that is the ones of whose citizens pressed such ideas, felt they didn't have "enough" – "enough of what?" Hatim had reflected – and there had been strange frictions at the borders like thin lines of fire in the brush. Recently, two Watchmen (men and women who traditionally walked the borders of the countries to keep the borderlines "official") had fought all night long over the carcass of a deer. The reputation of the Watchmen was always that of affection and good friendship and they were known for telling each other good stories when they met. They were continuously retold deep into the interior and spoken of as The Stories of the Watchmen. They were often funny and might carry a teaching.

Of this incident, it was generally reported that deer had become scarce in the area for the first time in history and so with that explained the occurrence away. Yet another report, generally overlooked, mentioned random changes in the weather that created a scarcity of deer, but emphasized a slow and serious decline in the values of the Watchmen, in the men and women themselves.

As they raced down the stairway, Hatim reflected that maybe Tanya had become a little too excited for a scientist. He couldn't understand why the make up of air could engender violence, but as they went out the door of the Institute and were confronted by a guard, simplicity asserted itself and Hatim was ready.

"Shhhhh," said Tanya to the guard. "We're playing a trick on the Director." She smiled brightly and the guard, confused, lowered his weapon to let them pass.

At that moment, through an upper window, the Director screamed, "Stop them, they are robbing the King."

Hatim relieved the dull guard of his weapon, and his breath, with a short punch to the solar plexus. He and Tanya jumped into a nearby buggy hitched with a team of fine, white horses. The occupants, a woman, who without hesitation, became hysterical, and her fat dog who immediately took a liking to Hatim and licked him full across the face. Hatim grimaced, took up the reins, and the horses were off at a wild gallop. The woman screaming at the top of her lungs and the fat dog, now in Hatim's lap, alternated between licking Hatim and sort of smiling a dog smile at Tanya. Defenseless, with the reins of the galloping horses in his hands, Hatim screamed to Tanya above the din.

"Take the damn dog!"

But Tanya who held both pails of milk, ignored him and indicated with her eyes that he should watch the road.

Like angels making plans for the world of men they sat under a coal black sky full of stars before a campfire of cedar sticks and talked of what could be done. They had abandoned the woman and the dog but the buggy stood alone polished in the starlight, and the fine white horses rested at the edge of the meadow.

Tanya explained to Hatim the intricacies of oxygen and he listened and understood.

"We will go to the King of Kaintuckee and tell him what we know," said Tanya.

"But he is only one King," replied Hatim.

"One King who understands could be enough," said Tanya. Hatim stirred the fire.

In the morning they rode on. The white horses pulled them with ease and the buggy was comfortable and snug. They talked about the King of Kaintuckee and how they might reach him.

The rumor and the reputation of the King was that he was a good and thoughtful ruler, but that his chief advisor told him only what he wanted him to hear, did wrong in his name, and was a wall of protection around the person of the King. Black-hearted and self-seeking, the chief advisor had a hold on the workings of the treasury, and worked the records of accounts to his favor. He was nicknamed: "Live or Die" for the power he had and it was widely wondered why the King could not see and understand. A story was that the chief advisor had saved the life of the King's son during an expedition into the interior and gratitude the King felt blocked his ability to monitor or know all his chief spokesman devised so cleverly.

The city was beautiful and open, designed for living: hanging vines and flowers, curves in the streets that were pleasing to the eye, walkways with soft grottos, running water and benches, and all around a great bazaar where the people met to buy and sell and talk, where the children played hopscotch and kick the can.

The King's palace was on a hill in the North. The palace was not extravagant but was distinguished by an architect of great understanding. There was color everywhere to make the eyes fall in love. Tanya pulled the horses to a halt outside the palace gate. She called a boy and asked him if he would like to water the horses to make some money and he was glad to have the work. There was no time to waste.

As Tanya and Hatim approached the gate, from a side door the chief advisor himself stepped forward – tall, heavy, with a furrowed brow – followed by guards. He pointed a thick finger and the guards surrounded and tied Hatim and Tanya with ropes. He eyed them, and then spoke quietly.

"I am Loadar, the King's understanding, and you are enemies of the state. Say goodbye to life itself. If you had not been so attached to your horses and buggy, I might not have known you, since your appearance reminds me of children who merely play games in the street."

"Playing games with children in the streets is my pleasure," said Tanya coldly.

At that Loadar disappeared into the palace.

The dungeon was lit with smoking torches, but the stone was not damp. Silence and emptiness lay upon the air. Their cell was made of stone. No human was near, but the young guard who stood at the door looking lonely, day dreaming of his girl and when they would meet after work was through. A dead dragon was etched in the stone wall and made colorful with dyes. Next to the dragon was a knight unfinished. The artist, thought Hatim, must have been taken away before he could draw the shield, the sword and the eyes. The knight seemed to be involved in some movement but no longer took interest in the dragon.

"We must get through the walls," said Tanya with a half smile.

"True," said Hatim taking his eyes from the unfinished knight. "Let's see what the guard is like."

"Guard," said Hatim roughly through the bars.

"Yes, sir," said the sleepy guard as he pulled himself from his thoughts.

"Loadar said to wait ten minutes and then release us. Did you get the instructions correctly?"

"He did?" replied the young guard with surprise.

"What! Have you been sleeping? Ten minutes is up."

"No, no," said the guard. "Don't try to fool me. Loadar didn't say anything to me. I haven't seen him, only his guards."

"He told the dumb one with the ears to tell you. Did he?"

"I'm not letting you out," said the guard.

"Who drew the dragon on the wall?" asked Hatim.

"The architect who designed this palace."

"Why?" asked Hatim briskly.

"No one knows. But they say he came alone here to

make the drawings and would let no one come with him."

"Why didn't he finish it?"

"That is the mystery," said the guard. "And there is one in every cell, all the same."

Hatim turned back to Tanya. She took his hand as if to bring them closer for a moment, as if it were needed.

"I know who designed this palace," she said. "He was known for his generosity and sense of beauty. He helped many people in his life. There must be a reason for this strange painting."

"The knight has no eyes," said Hatim. "And his head is turned away from the dragon."

"Let's see, if he had eyes, where would he be looking?"

"Here," said Hatim.

He put his hand on a triangular stone in the wall, unlike any other, but solid, unmovable. Both of them tried its edges. Then Tanya saw something, a bit of color, a bit of red. She asked Hatim for his boot and with the heel scraped at the stone. As the crust broke and crumbled, a tiny sword was revealed, perfect, as small as a needle, with red jewels in the handle. It pointed in a straight path across the cell to a square stone, exactly square, unlike the others, and when Hatim scraped it with his boot heel, there in the stone was a tiny shield, exact, shining like water. He pushed the stone. It moved!

Tanya threw her arms around Hatim and held him closely to her. Her long, golden hair covered her shoulder, her breasts softened the touch between them, and her sensitive fingers traveled along his back. "Oh, Hatim, Hatim."

The guard coughed like a rip in the air. Hesitantly they parted.

Hatim pushed the stone which slid slowly away and swung out with the precision of watch works tooled by a master. In moments they were through the opening into the unknown interior with the stone back in its place. There were slivers of space in the high wall that let in light. It shone directly on a message carved in a slab of stone:

You have done it, my Friend,
Keep to your resolve,
To the left leads out of the palace,
To the right the King's chamber,
May your wish be fulfilled,
May in seeking you be found.

Hatim lifted one hand palm open to the left and one to the right. He looked at Tanya for guidance.

"To the King's chamber," she whispered.

Hatim's eyes questioned for a moment, but only for a moment.

In the wall of the King's chamber they had a view through a design carved in stone. This design, an unknown door with hidden hinges, the view through the petals of leaves, the blooms of flowers, the edges of the moon, the arms of maidens, the feathers of the nightingale. They could see the entire chamber. The King was on the throne with Loadar beside him. Many people were gathered in the hall, friends and those seeking audience, ministers of state, family, employees, and some jugglers and acrobats who had come to perform.

There was a din of voices and laughter. The King was talking quietly and kindly to his son, a boy of about twelve who leaned casually against the throne. He had the look of a happy child, well-balanced and at ease. Suddenly, Loadar's voice boomed above the crowd. "Come to order," he thundered formally. "Let things begin..."

"Things began a long time ago," said the court jester near the throne, but only the King's son heard it and put his hand over his mouth to contain his laughter. Everyone became silent and faced the throne for the day's activities to start.

"Now," said Tanya.

They lifted the latch of the great design and it swung silently on its hidden hinges. Hatim and Tanya walked calmly out with the bearing of royalty, as if magically from nowhere. All eyes watched them, mouths went slack, some smiled. Some thought it was a surprise of the King. Loader stepped forward with fire in his eyes.

"Seize them. They have escaped the dungeon. They are enemies of the King."

The King looked at Loadar, surprised.

"I know of no one in the dungeon."

The guards moved forward.

Hatim put his arm around Tanya and spoke in powerful voice.

"We are friends of the King and bring him news of his Kingdom. And too, we know the secret of the dragon and the knight with no eyes."

"Hold," commanded the King to the guards. He stood tall, his colorful robe alive with his movement. He looked at Loadar grimly, and then: "Come forward," he said. "You who have escaped the dungeon."

Hatim and Tanya walked forward and when near stopped and bowed slightly as was the custom of respect.

"First, the news of my Kingdom, for that may be important to all of us. I will hear your words and I will see."

Loadar composed himself darkly with folded arms, sure of victory, but waiting for the moment to snatch it up. The guards kept their eye on him for a command. The jugglers lounged with the acrobats against the wall and the great hall was silent.

"Oh, King," said Hatim. "What we have to tell you will take reflection to believe enough to explore. It is born in science but in words is not perfect."

"I will reflect," said the King. Hatim and Tanya smiled in thanks.

"My name is Hatim Jones. I am but an engineer who maps the rain forests, some of which form a portion of your Kingdom. I will let my friend, my new friend, speak for both of us. Sire, this is Tanya. She is a woman of high and impeccable standards, a scientist in her own country. I present her to you as a ray of hope.".

"You are young, also," said the King, addressing Tanya sternly. She stepped forward, standing straight as was her habit, her golden hair rolling off her shoulders, her jeweled eyes catching the sunlight from a high window.

"Oh, King, it is true that I am young, but should that create disfavor? Fortune has made me one of the elite in the Science of Recovery, and in that position I am one of those who works half and half – intellect and intuition have their balance within me."

"Oh," said the King showing a glimmer of interest. "There are few of you left I understand."

Loadar raised his thick arm.

"Sire, if you will permit me," he broke in with a threatening voice. "There are few left, it is said, but only because they never existed in the first place. Time and research has shown them to be false, only cultists who took advantage of the gullibility of the people. There are many papers written."

"I am aware of the papers, Loadar," the King replied politely. "But it is my own experience that there may be something in it, I've had that feeling...." He frowned. "However, maybe it has no place in science."

"Our time is short," Loadar replied.

"Short, Loadar? Why are we here if not to have time? The woman has been courteous and we should hear her wish."

"She is wanted in her country, both of them are. They escaped detention for treason. They are stalling, dangerous. I can give you the details later, it is a complicated plan to undermine the economy."

The King frowned and leaned back on the throne.

"First, Tanya," said the King sternly. "If you were wanted in your own country, it is likely that I will return you there, but first tell your own story. Loadar, please wait."

"Oh, King," Tanya said. "Thank you for your patience. It is strong, I can tell. But I can also tell that your trust in intuition is not perfect. If you will permit, I would like to communicate with you in a rather unusual manner in order to bolster that trust."

"Speak," said the King.

"I would have your son speak for me."

The great hall burst into a din of murmuring and shuffling of feet. A small, red ball slipped from the hand of a nervous juggler and rolled silently like a tiny, crimson planet across the empty center of the chamber.

The boy, who still leaned against the throne, interested inall that was happening, genuinely happy, had been watching Tanya and Hatim intently. He liked them and as children will, had been unconsciously smiling as they spoke. Tanya was aware of him from the beginning, and in the force of her deeper perception had immediately realized his good nature and intelligence and the unusual purity of his state. He was now smiling more brightly at their attention.

“Explain,” said the King sharply to Tanya.

“It is very simple,” said Tanya. “Your son will speak and silently from where I stand I will impart to him the understanding of what to say. He will express it in his own way for the most part. I cannot impress this on him. It will only work if he wants it, likes it, and agrees.

The King glanced at Loadar.

“The people are restless, dismiss her,” said Loadar.

“But think about it, Oh, King,” said Tanya. “It is not perfect. Such a demonstration has no lasting value. It is the content I wish to impart and leave with you. I only offer this as sort of an advertisement for intuition. Personally, I could care less for such phenomena.”

“But why my son?”

“It is only a possibility because of the fine upbringing your son has been fortunate to have with you and your family, not in material things but in feeling, and because the contamination of disturbed thought has not touched him. May God grant him a long life without that touch.”

“Please, Father,” the boy said. “I like the lady. Let me try it. It could not hurt me.”

The King leaned forward. He looked at Loadar, at Tanya, then at Hatim and frowned. Hatim was looking at Tanya, then at Hatim and frowned. Hatim was looking at Tanya in disbelief.

“Hatim Jones,” said the King. “You seem puzzled.”

“Well,” said Hatim with a gulp. “She and I only recently met and I’ll have to admit she’s full of surprises. I guess I am interested too, though I would probably just tell you and get it over with." Tanya was smiling brightly at Hatim. The King understood Hatim's confusion and felt the tenderness between the two young people and he too smiled, but he was not softened.

"Please, Father," the boy said as he stepped out in front of the throne. Let me tell you her story."

"All you have to do," said Tanya to the boy. "Is take a deep breath and then another and look at your father; think that you love him, and then for a moment think of nothing."

Before the King could object, his son began to take slow, deep breaths, and the sight of his son's calmness smoothed him, he relaxed against the throne again with its spherical emblem mounted on the high back like an empty mandala.

Tanya, with no visible change in her demeanor, calmly looked a little to the side and downward.

'Father," the boy began, as naturally as he always talked to his father, "a few days ago this lady discovered the make-up of air. Air is not a substance of itself as we have always believed. It has components and the most interesting to us at this time is oxygen. The term is an old one, used one hundred thousand years ago before the destruction. It is a word recovered but never matched with its meaning until now. Tanya discovered it in her work for her government and members of that government have tried to suppress the knowledge because of certain corollaries to its function.

"Father, when you work with recovery, one center piece, as in a puzzle, can bring many pieces immediately together in a clear picture. This is what happened when Tanya discovered oxygen."

"Briefly – and later in the laboratory she will demonstrate this to you and our scientists – oxygen is the part of air that sustains us when we breath. When a person dies and there is no life the breathing stops; we know that. But chemically it is oxygen which is the main force to make us live.

"Strangely though, in plants oxygen is not used but given off, expelled, as we expel another substance when we exhale. Plants have no interest in keeping the oxygen. All around us the plants, in their own way, are breathing. Just like the green vines hanging above your throne, Oh, Father."

There was a murmur in the hall. A child's voice was heard from the back complaining to his mother. The King glanced up at the vines and then to his son.

"Are you all right, son," the King asked as if he were ready to halt the demonstration.

"I am fine, Father. It is pleasant telling these things." The King hesitated, unsure.

"This will be as brief as possible, Father. The substance we give off when we exhale is $CO_2$. Tanya has not yet deciphered the word that with "C", but $CO_2$ is our waste product. Yet it is what the plants take in, the trees if you will, like those in our rain forests, Father. $CO_2$ sinks into our two great rain forests and is metabolized, like food in our body, and oxygen is given off – this is nature, Father, in its beauty and its balance.

"Yet we have been and still are cutting millions and millions of acres of these wondrous forests every year; it has become part of the make-up of our economies to do so. At the same time our mechanical functioning, especially in the Northern Kingdoms, is producing billions of tons of $CO_2$ per year. Father, the whole world will begin to see the effects when the trees are not there to metabolize.

A $CO_2$ imbalance in the equatorial atmosphere of the planet has begun. This imbalance increases and enhances the heat retaining mechanism in the atmosphere of our Great Desert. Also, the heat energy that is deflected by $CO_2$ in the upper atmosphere creates violent winds which affect the lower atmosphere and becomes a primary cause of the spread of barrenness. And so it goes. We all know of the droughts, the people dying, the dry winds. It will spread, as dust spreads, to affect our planet. Hatim Jones, who now stand before you, a keen observer, will later discuss with you what he believes to be noncyclical changes in the weather."

The King leaned forward to speak.

"Please, Father, a few more words to finish the skeleton of Tanya's story."

"Continue," said the King formally, his eyes hardened.

"in cutting these forests what else could be the undiscovered outcomes that she had not yet considered. When we consider the balanced way the earth is put together, common sense would hint danger in extreme manipulations such as this. And further though it is a new and speculative field, cosmic particles of many descriptions rain upon our earth and interact with the molecules of matter. What is the cosmic pattern and its partnership with the great ocean of trees? Or just think of oxygen itself: the waste of the rain forests is a treasure of our being."

The boy walked back to his place and leaned against the throne as before. Yet his face was brighter, enhanced with energy as he looked at Tanya, so beautiful before the King.

The King turned to him. "Son, are you all right?"

"I'm fine, Father."

"Is she still speaking through you?" The King glanced at Tanya who had lifted her gaze from where she held it and had assumed her former demeanor, waiting with respect before the King.

"No, Father, she's not, and though I didn't understand much of what she said, I'd like to know what we'll do with the forests gone where you and I explore."

"This is insane," roared Loadar. "A side show, magic tricks, babblings of the treasonous. She desires the crumbling of our economy and your rule."

The people all over the great hall began to murmur and then shouts broke out as they began to take sides. A fight started and a crowd surrounded it, shouting insults and opinions.

The King stood, snatched up his tall, wooden staff and brought it down hard on the floor.

'Silence," commanded the King and his guards repeated it. Like a wave from the throne to the back of the room the hall grew quiet. In that moment, Tanya spoke:

"It was to get this knowledge to you, Oh, King, that I escaped my country for some there wished to suppress it, and it was for this reason we were thrown in your dungeon by Loadar."

"And for that reason they will go back," boomed Loadar. "My guards, seize them to protect your King."

"Stop," cried the King. "They are now my guests to be listened to." Loadar's guards hesitated.

"Seize," shouted Loadar. "Seize them now. It is I who need to explain to you, Oh King." The guards moved forward.

"Stop," commanded the King. Loadar was blinded with rage.

"Seize them and seize the King," cried Loadar. "He needs protection. The woman is speaking through him."

The King spun deftly and with his carved, wooden staff caught Loadar across the front of his knees a heavy blow so that bones were heard to crack across the chamber.

"My guard," commanded the King. "Seize Loadar's men."

Hatim, in that moment took the forward two of Loadar's guards and with handfuls of hair popped their heads together twice and let them fall stunned to the floor.

It was over. The King stood calmly holding his staff. Loadar lay ineffectively on the floor, and Tanya smiled a smile that spread so fully to all who saw it, that the violence was dissipated and a feeling of grace shone on the faces and in their being. Even the King showed a subtle, relaxed smile as he surveyed the expanse of his chamber.

"If you listen to them," snarled Loadar from the floor. "Poverty will sweep your Kingdom like a dry wind."

"In that case," said the King. "We will tighten our belts and seek work where we can. What is a Kingdom to a planet?"

The people were arguing among themselves, taking a side, according to their interests and the conditioning of their minds, so the King dismissed them from the Chamber. Hatim took Tanya's hand and slowly she leaned into his arms and her lips brushed his neck for a long moment. The King waited, then cleared his throat politely.

"Before we rest," said the King as he put his arm warmly around his son who had stepped up beside him. "You say you know the secret of the knight with no eyes. My curiosity is strong. What is that secret?"

Tanya had a feeling as she had looked at the circular stone above the King's throne. She remembered the square stone and the triangular stone and realized that the round one would make the full three. She asked Hatim for his boot. Hatim, puzzled again, smiled and took it off.

"Always full of surprises," he said to the King.

Tanya approached the throne and with the heel of Hatim's boot scratched away the crust on the circular stone until revealed were two bright blue eyes, clear, and finely tooled with polished jewels of all the many colors to make the shadings of light. The eyes were as if real, glittering, at ease.

Tanya turned and smiled while the eyes stared at them over her shoulder full of peace and understanding.

"Here is the final secret of the Knight," she said. "His eyes, his vision, always there, but often hidden, full of wisdom and chivalry for the world. They are the real eyes of the King and the King's son, and they are my eyes and Hatim's. They are clear and they see. Full of all that is good, all that is positive, they contain the upward leading sense: of generosity, of trust, of perception and peace, they go toward and receive from the ultimate force of our universe. They are not ponderous. There is purity there and gratitude for the gift of life."

All stood quietly in the silence until Tanya spoke again:

"And one more thing," she said. "The trees are only the basic, the planet only the foundation. Get the problems cleared up and forget about them. All this is a nuisance. There is something else carried on the air, invisible and immeasurable. That is why I am really here. It is the element of all brightness, in the sky, in your eyes and in the eyes of the stones… and the sticks. When people experience that, they will be able to truly use the air; they will know what it really means to take a breath."

The King looked at Hatim with pleasure.

"She is full of surprises," he said.

He then granted Hatim and Tanya free access to his palace and his entire Kingdom, and decreed that when they were married they would be the heirs to the throne in preparation for his own son who would follow in time.

Since it is not necessary to demand cause and effect in the same story, it is enough to say that the problem of the waste of the rain forests was presented.

And the pails of milk? That is simple. On the journey to the palace, Tanya, though not hungry, made sure that Hatim drank it before it spoiled!

NOTE: This story was sent out by Hatim to all the other Kingdoms and beamed out through the galaxy by technology developed during his reign. Some correspondence read as follows:

From the Kingdom:

1. "King Hatim, did you and your Queen Tanya actually experience the events of this narrative or was it devised solely as a communication?"

Hatim replied: "Does it matter?"

2. "King Hatim, we could have been sympathetic to many of the claims made in this document if it had not been for the 'intuitive factors' and 'factors of invisibility' and such which it contained. Do you really think they have validity."

Hatim replied: "Yes".

3. "King Hatim, it is our opinion that the narrative related to us is shallow, child-like and without substance and a waste of time. We further feel that such a story is

beneath the standards of a King."

Hatim replied: "Thank you. I'll try again."

4. "King Hatim, we have received your communications. Let us know what we can do to help you in your endeavor."

King Hatim replied: "Thank you, I will."

There was one reply from a planet the location of which is not yet deciphered:

5. "King Hatim, we are not like you. Not in the structure of our life nor in language. Our situation is different and we have no rain forests."

King Hatim replied: "What do you have?"

# The Fall Night

The fall night
Brushed stars
Together or apart
We breathe

# A Strange Camp in a Wild Garden

(In Honor of Rain)

All the beautiful horses were in the green fields grazing or standing under the trees with head down and a back leg unlocked, resting. Chestnut, white, brown, sorrel, paint, buckskin, palomino, bay, black and gray – each with a name and a way of being, always charm there and wildness – horses that looked to me and looked to my Mother in times of care.

There is trust and a tender response which can develop between people and horses – depending on the people – depending on the horses. Some people prefer horses to people, but that was not our way. People can reason and they have the hidden capacity to consciously expand and direct the spirit. And with some there is a yearning within them to uncover that capacity. Horses are limited to the acceptance of their given nature and an acceptance of their life experience, undirected by them, that might adapt to this nature – good or bad. They look mostly to food, rest and procreation; and yet, awareness there. People don't usually do well when they limit their experience to that of horses. Horses do well as horses, with understanding people to help them live out of the wild.

Charm and beauty and love – my mother was charming, beautiful within and without, and she lived from the foundation of a tremendous love – a field of force coming naturally from her. That is what she strove for, that is what she chose to understand.

She was of medium stature and very straight in

her posture. Though not straight from effort only, but from vitality – and more than that: it was an inborn and cultivated energy that gave her the dynamic of a fine carriage. If you see Ruthie in an old photograph in black and white, and maybe the picture is crinkled and she is in a crowd, you will see something vibrant and engaging looking out at you from deep brown eyes. She loved people, respected them, and gave the hospitality of herself or her home with a shining and deep regard.

She recognized those who twinkled and those who struggled and gave each of them her very best – naturally – from her powerful nature, from the force of perception contained within her. Yet with those very deep in selfishness, greed, inconsiderate behavior, cruelty, foolishness, she could simply disappear. She could be tough and forthright (especially if it was family with this troubled behavior and she felt a duty to make an effort) and then disappear. She was never discourteous, as it were, as she knew it to be impractical and inappropriate. She sensed the people she must avoid, that was part of the context of her knowledge – it was not warmth by ritual. She gave each person what might bring harmony, if that is all they could take. If they could take more, she gave what could push them on in their growth – as one might clap their hands at a bird to give it the freedom out the opened window.

In those early days when I was a child in the late 1940s and 1950s, Scotland Farm was an earthly paradise. Just after I was born, my mother moved to the farm from the city. Not just any city, but a real city, Chicago! She had no background in country life, other than the buggy rides to a cabin by a creek when she was a young girl and with her own mother and father. Mother would wake me up and say in a lilting music:

"John, it's a new day!"

Her voice had the ring of inspiration and wonder, as that was where it came from, genuinely and deep, within her. Not only did I feel wonder, I felt secure; as secure, I think, as any being could be who knew internally that it was a shifting world. And from the tremendous lessons that came from a farm full of animals, insects, weather, work and very unusual people moving about like angels, or like some other form of human creatures in their different levels of light, I could see externally that it was a world not to be discounted too soon as simple.

Certain poetry was among all the creative impacts, and special stories too, and there was the slow learning of the deep meaning within courtesy and good manners.

Ruthie expressed beauty, as the old saying goes. She was fine to see – her inwardness made it so – something around the eyes and the bones of her cheeks, her energy that drew you in, made you feel better and true – not just form, but beauty in its finest sense: a refined action within.

She was not in love with mules or axes as happens with many men and some women in the country. Nor was she in love with food, as happens with a lot of men and a lot of women wherever you find them. She understood the foundations of these things, their necessity and use. She had no idols; she was not a cultist. She never intoned praises of food beyond a respect for doing it right: that is simple, and enhanced by the force of love that came from her being – she cooked from that place, with that concentration.

We ate simply. Meal time was a pleasure, a time that brought psychological and physical strength; we visited, we were renewed. Desserts now and then, but simply and sparingly – a little ice cream, and at special times, a Coke from the old, green bottles, opened pop-fizz on the wall and poured over the ice cream – a purple cow we called it. Sometimes we had it with Grapette, and as the grape flowed over the ice cream she would laugh and say, "Purple cow!" Then we would laugh like laughing with the wind.

We would often laugh heartily and long at the simplest turns of a word, or a thought that had no boundaries and seemed to live in the air: made for laughter, well beyond thinking. Whoever was with us (often one of my school friends who had come to visit) would be caught up too in the laughter, and in the end, quizzically look around as if it were all a joyous mistake, and with that we would all be laughing again, renewed by yet another flight beyond the literal and the mundane. We would sit at the table with the tall windows opened wide listening to the katydids and the crickets in the long, Kentucky summer nights. Warm air would sift through the windows or cool rain would fall.

And as for the mules or the big, paint workhorses – she wanted them cared for. I remember her leaning on the gate to the long, race barn in a summer dress and her ankle high shoes.

Ruthie expressed in her being that the best of women and men will want, and aspire to, beauty of the heart, a tenderness, and a sense of timing that makes each moment alive and full of spark and harmony.

Ruthie never complained, and I imagine many who came close to her, took her to their heart and imagination. I remember the way my father, who shared her characteristics of strength differently, kindly said her name in his resonant voice, as if the name were a poem itself, "Ruthie." He recognized her spell of love.

A year after I was born, Ruthie moved to the farm from Chicago. We had been living there in the hotel my father managed. He had inherited part of Scotland Farm from his own family, and bought the rest from his brothers. Farm life was new to her, and when some time had passed, she became a strong and willing worker.

I leaned there, too, looking through the slats of the gate, but quickly climbed up on the high rail. My father remained in Chicago; he would fly home every other Friday from his job – light years away, it seemed – to be with us on the farm.

It is around 1951 or 1952. My sister and brother have been in college for most of four or five years. They are married, living away, and have children of their own. I am about eight with an experienced mother at my side. The mules are comfortable and cool. They are in a twenty-stall barn alone eating hay. It is shady in the dusty lane that makes an oval around the barn.

Bill, who raised our tobacco, wears a straw hat and carefully pressed khaki shirt and trousers. In his shirt pocket is a pack of Lucky Strikes. There is an old mule and a young mule he will harness. Bill has just left the little service station down the road at Jett where he has been sitting on a chair out front talking, smoking and having a coke. He is robust and intelligent, his face is round and smooth, and he has a warm disposition. His profession as a tobacco farmer was a traditional one; he was good at it, and in those days, people smoked more innocently. Bill has waited until after the heat of the day to begin burning the tobacco beds.

"What's the news Bill?" Ruthie asks in her welcoming voice. She wants to know. She has a lot to consider, a lot to care for. She has a field of horses, mares, and a blind stallion in the stud barn. These are not expensive horses, but mares my Father would get as gifts from friends or cheaply here and there, horses that few people wanted, unusual horses with good breeding that just came to him, as he let things just come to him in his life. These great horses with beautiful names would come his way, and he would pass them on to my Mother to watch over – with names of Dusty Dream, Eternal Za, Myrtle Flynn, Cobbler's Honey, Lea, and Sing Lulu. I remember Sing Lulu as most alive, strong and watchful, with a long dark mane and tail and she was light on her feet; she was never really interested in the world around her – she seemed to look to some-thing else, always drinking it in. There were many others; I can see them now and feel my head against their shoulders.

She had two milk cows to consider, a herd of sheep, a good number of beef cows, chickens, geese, ducks, a border collie, an outdoor cat, some hounds, and a pet crow. Only the border collie came in the house; and too, in the house, the little weak lambs she brought into the kitchen and put in a cardboard box under the old, gas cook stove with legs. She would nurse the lambs back to health, and with Earl, who lived with his family on the farm and helped us in the early days, she would go to the barn and get the ewe to take the baby lamb back again and nurse it. This would sometimes be a process over a day or two, and now and then the ewe would refuse and the lamb would be raised on a bottle. Often the lamb was a weak twin or the victim of the unpredictable, and often fierce, Kentucky weather. A tablespoon of bourbon whisky from Ruthie's hopeful hands, squeezing open the lamb's mouth, would often be the first step to life for the little, soft lamb, limp and empty of strength.

She also had the care of the rough pony I rode, and

her own horse.

"Horses are like people," she once said. "They must be taught by one who knows what has to be done; they must be treated kindly. Son, it's not a small thing to be responsible for a young animal."

With dogs or horses or people she gave generously of her time and attention, and the earned experience of her flexible and brilliant mind. The intention was there too, love shone – she wanted to be true. Added to that, there was never a time that she felt complete in her knowledge; 'trial and error' was an accepted technique consciously applied, the outcome rarely forgotten. Humility (as it grew in her) was her foundation.

Earl came in to the barn from the other gate. The chain rattled as he latched it. He had been feeding Deliberator, the blind stallion, a dark bay with flowing mane, and a tail which brushed the ground. Deliberator knew the boundaries of his one pasture and our voices. Tender, sensitive beyond his eyes – in my heart he was a powerful force. I remember him running to me from the center of the field, wheeling around with both front feet off the ground, but contained, stopping at ease before the fence – just there.

"Morning Miss Hay, morning Earl."

Love is not wine from the bottle, but the same "wine of spirit" that flows in Ruthie. There is an inspiration to learn that grows in people, to understand the mind and the reality that surrounds us – to begin to know 'when' and 'how', or 'if' to act at all? To 'know' how it all really works.

The *Rubaiyyat* of the Sufi poet, Omar Khayyam, was always on a table somewhere in the house or at intervals at Ruthie's bedside, and sometimes Shakespeare (whose work she dipped in gently), and the Romantic poets, or the ancient Sufi writer Saadi, and the Arabian Nights stories, called the Mother of Records; those ancient middle eastern stories that have charmed all ages for hundreds and hundreds of years. Sometimes she had the Richard Burton translation of the Arabian Nights there, or another translation; a large rich and worn book with drawings – exotic, romantic, wild or tender, showing wise men, fools, jinn, and lovers in an embrace of tender truth.

There were collections of poetry, and she would often go back to the same poems year after year, reading them aloud to me, stopping me as I passed – always with the same sparks of love and inspiration in her eyes when she looked up at me after the last line – always saying, often in words, always in her being:

> "We struggle, but this is a lovely world, there is a romantic mystery – Son, be grateful, learn, be joyful, love."

Ruthie acted from some inner sense at the time in her life that I knew her. She served, she served greatly, but she didn't serve abstractions or 'issues' of society or religion that someone had conditioned into her brain. She sensed religion in and beyond the mundane, and she served what was there to serve – in a practical way – as she struggled and loved her days.

To know 'when' and 'how' and 'if' to act at all was part of the growing fabric of her intuition. With people on all levels of society, decisions are usually based in intellect, emotion, and conditioning. Those responses, often false, are conditioned routinely into the brain and body by family, friends, school, and the culture as a whole. In a time of so called 'issues', a phrase can throw people into a flurry of doing what they think of as 'good' or 'right'. But Ruthie's "being" asks: what is truly appropriate, and when, and with whom, and what is the method? This is part of the mystery that she always sought directly from her heart, which transformed and expanded the spiritual heart's delicate substance.

On the farm, there was so much to do of a practical nature, and so much natural and ongoing preparation. And yet, mistakes were made and struggles were there. As I remember, however, with Ruthie there was some kind of smoothness in that rough journey. As it is said, associate with those who are 'lucky', on whom fortune shines, and find that much will be silently 'understood' by you.

Later in life, Ruthie laughed with the ancient, eastern teaching stories of Nazrudin's doings, and I enjoyed telling the stories, ones I gathered from the books that collected them. In the stories, he was always a comic character. Just the mention of his name and we would begin to laugh. We laughed not so much at the jokes involved, but at the inexpressible thing the stories did in the mind, and, as always, it was usual for us to laugh. Laughter was a part of life on the farm. My mother, father and I were exploring the timber of their mind and the minds of all the other characters, old and young, strong or timorous, growing up in that green garden.

One day Nazrudin was at his home getting some things done around the house. A busy body came running in calling:

"Nazrudin, Nazrudin, the woman next door is baking bread!"

"What is that to me," Nazrudin replied.
"But Nazrudin, she's going to give you some."
"What is that to you," said Nazrudin.

On the farm, there was a lot of that: when to do what, when and with whom, and where, in a natural way, to fit in rhythm; and, finally, what is your timely connection with the functioning of truth. And with our life there, it was not so much spelled out, but inspired: that which is 'given' at another level.

In some very clear way farming wasn't what it was about, though its pressures were great. Is life ever about the physical endeavor only? It wasn't merely a farm – it was a paradise, green and strange, dangerous and a delight. It was made for the mind and the spirit. The house was large. There wasn't much furniture. There was an open fire in winter and a breeze in summer, and minds attuned to making truthful things happen. We lived comfortably and very simply. We didn't think overly much of style, clothes or possessions.

My father, later, in admiration for beauty, began buying stray antiques for a song, but none of us cared in the usual egocentric sense. My father was a strong and sensitive man. He was sensitive to his care for us. In the 50 years I knew him, he never said an unkind word to me, nor did my mother, not one. He expressed, in his living, tenderness and strength. He was gentlemanly. Yet, let him be the subject of another time.

Life there was eternal, as we didn't feel the time, yet in our hearts it was fleeting – a strange camp in a wild garden. All was isolated and quiet, moonlit, or covered in black night, white, white stars, no sound but an owl or the passing train near the far field. Lying in bed alone

I would think, "Someday I'll be on that train." If it was winter, white and frozen, and after the train, all would be quiet again, and I would lie there at the very end of time, protected and alone. We all wandered there, my mother, father and I, with and without each other, all alone, preparing for and seeking out the good.

Life there was eternal as we didn't feel the time, yet in our hearts it was fleeting – a strange camp in a wild garden.

I remember the over-ripe pears on the ground under the tree by the smoke house, a tree that seemed so old that climbing in it I always found branches to break off and throw to the ground. I had seen my father jump high and break dead branches from trees with the weight of his body. If it were a heavy branch, for a moment he would be suspended, etched against the landscape, still, until the loud crack when he would land on his feet, limb in hand, or land to dodge with churning legs and shielding arms the fall of some tremendous branch. In the very old days, before our family owned it, when the farm was several thousand acres, there were orchards. This pear tree and one other, and the few apple trees left scattered about, were descendants of those old trees: delicate varieties, fruit crisp and delicious, unheard of now in the marketplace. I would walk down to get a pear or an apple with a friend from town. We would stand quietly in the shade to eat it. We might pick up one or two for Mother, but it was casual like that. Others would stop under the trees and eat in season as well.

The books that mother cherished brought sparks of understanding to us all. It is strange that among those few books, that touched the ineffable in her, were several from the eastern Sufi tradition. The hundreds of books in the dark attic and in the chests and shelves around the house were left over from an earlier generation, many from the Victorian era. In that era, with the translation of Omar Khayyam's *Rubaiyyat*, writings of that ancient, eastern flavor were very popular – there was something felt if not fully understood in that fresh thinking, or we might say, in the mysterious packaging of that unencumbered thought. Ruthie just found these books among the books left there by past generations, and maybe she knew them in her childhood, but it was not surprising that they were in our home; and yet, why does this depth of thinking toward the inner being last? What protects it? Why does such a woman as my mother hold to it? The story of life at Scotland Farm might tell.

And why did my bedtime stories, read aloud to me by Ruthie over a period of years, include the strange, inspired, often violent tales of the Blackfoot Indians (*Indian Why Stories, Sparks from War Eagle's Lodge-Fire*) – a book of stories found by her, of course, probably on one dark rainy day in the great, crowded attic – in the attic were hundreds of books, a witch's hat, hoop skirts, old chests, letters, wind, and a variation on the timeless silence that infused our busy lives.

The book of *Indian Why Stories* was left in my room where often I stared at the captivating illustrations by Charles Russell, of animals and Indians and landscapes. I might look into the tales myself; and I pondered uncomfortably over such places in the human mind. Old Man, the central character, was a trickster, a thief, a death dealer, and one who simply made the animals what they were. Yet, he was other things too in his primitive travels to help define the natural world for young Indians: he struggled and he wondered. For us, Ruthie and I, there was a longing felt in the stories as well, the possibility of innocence gained, of truth attained, of something beyond the troubles and evil of the world, even beyond its false limits or false freedoms which enforce boredom and lethargy. These stories were designed to make a young Indian grow up and survive in a simpler world, and often to believe literally. For Ruthie and me, they made their blend with other stories, other cultures, detachment, other tracks of time.

I was seven or eight, and the stories imposed a darker world that was not my own. And yet, by that age, I had 'heard', and they had been 'told' to me, that is told by Ruthie, my father, in the adventures of the Cisco Kid, the Lone Ranger, Earl, the horses in the field, the weather, Billy Goat Gruff, Bomba, Tarzan, my schoolmates, and by that age I had felt, as well, that Old Man lives within the minds of people. The impact of the stories was fierce, but romantic. These few lines, a poem of mine, that follow won't well describe Old Man at all; he was a tougher, simpler bird, but the poem could describe, in part, the beginnings of a longer evolution Old Man might facilitate or inspire. Could it be the evolution of War Eagle, from whose lodge the stories of Old Man came, or Ruthie's evolution, or my own.

Whispers –
Only a child
At last in tenderness,
I grew up with a bold and ancient warrior,
Limber he was, and beautiful in his looks of wonder,
And though having lived, he was a child too
In his earthly travels for knowledge

His only narcotic.
Curious he was, his eyes light as sun rays,
Slow to anger, sure to wander off,
Ambitious in his search for nothing.
A fist ready for the event of evil,
And one hand out in love, as pure as leaf.
And yes, I grew up with him,
Only a blonde and delicate child
Who would stand in the path for hours,
One hand holding the other.
He touched my dreams with his daring
And all his chances in such a dangerous world,
With the softness of his eyes in innocent victory,
With his lone patience in the long nights tending wounds so deep,
Near a campfire small enough to break my heart.
I fell often for having known him,
Became brave, hear the whispers,
With no way to dodge the imprint
Of his bright shiver among the trees.

Or she would read from many of the old books of adventure and good deeds. After reading to me, we would say the Lord's prayer which she had taught me, and which had been taught to her as a child. When I was very small I knelt beside her, and a little later on she let me lie under the covers, against the cold, to pray out loud with her, and later she would just remind me, sweetly, "Don't forget your prayers, son." And later, while I was still very young, she left it to me. Nothing that implied a greater world was ever imposed. She wanted me to feel prayer, but somehow it was never a reverence apart from the way we lived our lives at Scotland, but a fitting expression of gratitude to close the day. Nor was it an exact meaning of words that mattered, but as if there was, very near, something tremendous and invisible and holy, if you will, that made things happen. And it was being quietly near Ruthie, a beautiful and capable woman, who obviously respected the essence in it without fear or pathos. And it was another sense, and encouragement, that there was more to life than Old Man could let on.

And when our prayer ended we blessed everyone.

When we are children we might experience directly that which is creative and true, unspoken, connected on a deeper level. But then it is mixed up with all that is around us: people, words, material. That mix is what we know, often even, what we become forever. Our experience is not, then, broad enough to filter out, to be detached, to reject, to walk away, or finally to be impervious on a deeper level to the disturbance and trash of the world, or, to be impervious to the thoughts and actions which affect the mind negatively and in a counter-evolutionary manner. Someone should be there to help the child, someone who knows.

Little children – their struggles could be lightened if adults had the intention to make themselves something unusually strong and perceptive inside so they could then help children and others. But adults might not have the intention or the knowledge or even the idea of what could be done; they can be like children, too – operating in the old damage without really changing. Yet, there are those that have an inkling of this, who change later – usually those who have suffered long with an understanding that didn't work, a false understanding that only brought unhappiness and decline.

Yet, there are adults who have true direction and

pure inspiration, who have a balance in their struggles, and are able to pass it on. Some might make a leap of intuition and change beyond even their best teachers, and some might have teachers who have become, in their brief stay on earth, equal to anything that can be done within.

When Ruthie's father, Ben Williams, a young and vital seventy-year old went fly fishing one morning on Elkhorn Creek, he thought it might rain. The creek was shallow with clear water rushing over the rocks, not too wide, and a green radiance from the canopy of trees that covered, and the white marble of the sycamore bark decorated the bank. Trim in his build, wearing hip boots and vest and old hat, he fished the creek gracefully even after the wind began to blow and the temperature dropped and the rain and wind began to ruffle and spot the creek. He probably liked the weather coming and felt it against him, and loved the outdoors then as he always did, even though the fish would not now be biting.

He had ten children; two had died young – and Ruthie, the youngest remaining, now a young bride gone to California with two children of her own. Being the youngest of so many, and with a spirit so strong, she had a lot of behavior to look to and learn from, and had an advantage of being down the line for a little freedom to explore. And too, she had parents who had matured.

When the rain began to fall in sheets and soak his clothes, Ben Williams rolled in his line with the blue feathered fly and walked back through the fields for the long drive home. But somehow he caught a cold which turned into pneumonia. There was no penicillin then. He died very quickly. When he was dying, he called for Ruthie. I want to see Ruthie. She was the one he called for. And when he became a little delirious he called. "Where is Ruthie, where is Ruthie, little Ruthie?"

She was in California, a long way from Kentucky, and it was 1927, and travel, even by plane, was expensive and difficult. One of the sisters pretended to be Ruthie in those last moments, and held his hand. Ruthie loved him closely from afar.

Change is just there; we might be confused. We often complain about change. It destroys our equilibrium; it makes us worry. What does it interrupt? It interrupts expectations, it interrupts the limits of what we can conceive. It interrupts desire.

Suppose that change could be accepted. Just suppose that change could be worked with always in the attitude of a loving and patient parent, a parent engaged with the rhythms of spirit?

A clock chimes from the steeple and
There is no breaking,
A train shakes all the earth around us
And there is no breaking.
A visitor comes and then another spilling dry words
Shuffling dry heels and coughing –
But that opening accepts no breaking.
Call me if you will on a thousand phones
Whisper my name at the little window
Listen to the color of the white gardenia,
The yellow zinnia, the ivory nasturtium,
There will be no breaking –
Only love.

Made in the USA
Columbia, SC
01 February 2023

11384855R00104